THE BIG BOOK OF EGYPTIAN MYTHOLOGY

THE BIG BOOK OF EGYPTIAN MYTHOLOGY

CLAUDIO BLANC

Camelot
EDITORA

Copyright © 2021 Claudio Blanc
Rights reserved and protected by law 9.610 of 2.19.1998.
No part of this book may be reproduced, filed in a search engine or transmitted by any means, whether electronic, photocopy, recording or others, without prior authorization from the rights holder, and may not be circulated, bound or covered in a different manner than that in which was published, or without the same conditions being imposed on subsequent buyers.
1st Edition 2021

President: Paulo Roberto Houch
MTB 0083982/SP

Editorial Coordination: Paola Houch
Translation: Francine Cervato
English translation review: Gareth Clough
Edition: Priscilla Sipans (redacao@editoraonline.com.br)
Graphic project: Rubens Martim (rm.martim@gmail.com)
Images: Shutterstock (except page 9 - Wikicommons/ Jeff Dahl).

Sales: Phone: +55 (11) 3393-7723
vendas@editoraonline.com.br

The legal deposit was made.

International Cataloging in Publication (CIP) According to ISBD		
C181b	Camelot Editora	
	The Big Book of Egyptian Mythology / Camelot Editora. - Barueri : On Line Editora, 2023. 144 p. ; 15,1cm x 23cm.	
	ISBN: 978-65-85168-56-4	
	1. Mythology. I. Title.	
2023-2052		CDD 292.13 CDU 292
Elaborated by Vagner Rodolfo da Silva - CRB-8/9410		

Rights reserved to
IBC — Instituto Brasileiro de Cultura LTDA
CNPJ 04.207.648/0001-94
Juruá Avenue, 762 – Alphaville Industrial
ZIP CODE. 06455-010 – Barueri/SP
www.editoraonline.com.br

Summary

Presentation 7

The Egyptian Civilization 11

The Dynasties 33

The Egyptian Religion 63

Cosmogonies 77

The Egyptian Gods 87

Bibliography 141

Presentation

The first civilizations arose in the Mesopotamia region, developing forms of government, legislation and writing, and then, fell into decay. Shortly after disappearing in Sumer, the first signs of civilization started breaking out in Egypt. Maybe this civilization could have been riginated or influenced by the Sumerians. It is not known, but it is speculated that this is likely. In any

Map of ancient Egypt, showing major cities and sites (c. 3100 – 30 BC.)

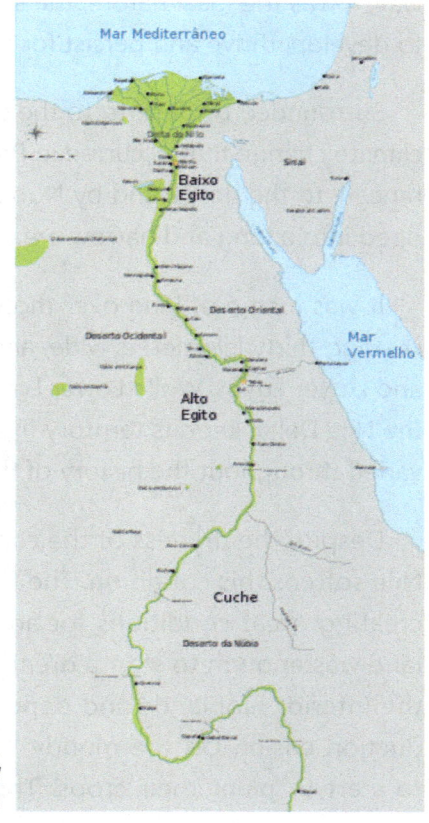

Characteristic landscape of the Nile.

way, it was the local nature, the scenery, which allowed this civilization to develop, thrive and persist for more than three thousand years.

Surrounded by deserts, to the east and west – which arose from the climate change that occurred in Prehistory –, delimited by the Mediterranean, to the north, and by Nubia, to the south, ancient Egypt developed into a long and narrow area, on the banks of the River Nile.

It was a strip of land over thousand kilometers long, but rarely exceeding thirty kilometers wide, and which naturally divided into Upper and Lower Egypt. While Lower Egypt, which corresponds to the area of the Nile Delta, kept its territory fixed, the southern limit of Upper Egypt varied throughout the history of this civilization.

Despite the dryness of the climate, especially in Lower Egypt, the Nile softens this condition. The floods of the river fertilize the banks, creating great conditions for agriculture. Thus, that narrow strip of land was enough to start a great civilization. The mud, brought from the interior highlands and deposited there, made agricultural production easier. On the muddy banks, the first Egyptians were able to start to plant their crops. Their land slowly turned into a long, isolated oasis, surrounded by deserts and mountains. It was a region of easy handling. The Egyptians did not need to carry out work to recover the land, and the Nile was a gentle river. Although it overflowed every year, it did so in a predictable way. Its floods were not sudden and destructive disasters. On the contrary, they were very regular, which allowed them to establish a pattern for the agricultural year. The Nile was like a clock, regulating the eternal cycles that moved the lives of the ancient Egyptians.

The occupation of this area occurred from the sixth millennium BC, receiving waves from different peoples. The ethnicity of the Egyptians results from the mixture of these human groups that, since prehistoric times, mixed with each other.

Around 3300 BC, a considerable number of people were already living along a strip of land of about five hundred kilometers on the Lower Nile, in villages and towns, close to each other. People organized themselves into clans and the cities took time to develop, probably because there was no threat of invaders. As a result of this, farmers

The "River of Life" secured the wealth of the Egyptian civilization (fishermen on the Nile).

did not need to take refuge in cities to protect themselves. It is known that these primitive Egyptians built reed boats, worked stone and used copper, turning it into utensils for daily use. In the middle of the fourth millennium, they started maintaining contact with other areas, especially Mesopotamia. From then on, starts what would constitute, over the centuries, the Egyptian civilization.

The Egyptian Civilization

The Egyptian civilization lasted more than three thousand years and had five main phases until it gradually disappeared under Roman rule, when Christianity came to be the religion of the Empire. The Egyptians developed a very complex civilization that worked efficiently during most of their three thousand years of history.

The god Ptah, patron of the city of Memphis and of artisans and architects, sitting on his throne, with the god Sekhmet behind him (Temple of Ramses II, Luxor, Egypt).

The Egyptian people were embodied in the State, established in Memphis, capital of the Old Kingdom. Later, in the New Kingdom, the capital was established in Thebes. Both cities were major religious centers and had a complex of palaces rather than an urban center properly said.

The Pharaoh

The State machine consisted of civil, ecclesiastical, and military authorities. However, the idea that the Egyptians had of the State was different from what we conceive today. They had less the concept of the State and more the idea of what belonged to the pharaoh and, to some extent, to the temples. The pharaoh, considered a deity, the incarnation of Horus, was a key figure, the center of Egyptian life. He was responsible for the continuity between the divine and the human, the cosmic and the social. During most of ancient Egyptian history, all social powers, even priestly authority, derived from the pharaoh and were delegated by him.

At an early stage, the Egyptian monarchs already possessed great authority, as the first monuments of this civilization testify. The divine aspect of the pharaoh originated with prehistoric "kings" who had a different role than later monarchs. These "kings" were holy men, re-

Death Mask of Tutankhamun, Egypt.

Depiction of the pharaoh Tutankhamun receiving flowers and papyri from Ankhesenamun.

sponsible for the health and prosperity of the land and the community that depended on it. It was believed that these kings – and the rites presided by them – ensured a good harvest, the absence of pests, and the fertility of women. In several prehistoric cultures, kings represented the Sun and had an entourage of twelve assistants, related to the solar months (the thirteen, the king and the entourage, referred to the lunar months). Usually, the king was sacrificed on the winter solstice, and one of the members of his entourage replaced him.

In Egypt, this belief subsisted, although modified, in the figure of the pharaoh. He was the one who controlled the annual floods of the Nile – which was equivalent to controlling the lives of communities that depended on the river. The first rituals under the pharaoh's responsibility were related to fertility, irrigation, and the recovery of the land. Depictions of Menes, the founder of Egypt, show him digging a canal.

However, in a civilization that extended for three thousand years, the idea of the king's divine nature had different meanings. The Egyptians recognized exceptional rulers and were aware that others were very weak. Thus, the belief in the pharaoh's divine nature did not interfere with the perception of his human aspect. In the Old Kingdom, it was considered that the monarchy and Egypt itself had a divine ori-

The colossal head of the pharaoh Ramesses, in the temple of Luxor, in Thebes, Egypt.

gin. The pharaoh became one of the manifestations of Horus, without, however, losing human characteristics. It was believed that justice was what the pharaoh loved, and evil, what he hated. He possessed divine omniscience and, therefore, did not need a code of laws to guide him.

In the Middle Kingdom, the pharaoh lost, to a certain extent, the divine powers of his role and started representing humanity before the gods. However, in the New Kingdom, the pharaoh started being considered physically the son of Horus, or Re, who had assumed the aspect of the king to generate in the queen the next pharaoh. At that time, he started being depicted with the heroic stature of the great warriors. They appear on monuments in their war chariots, crushing enemies or hunting wild beasts. JM Roberts quotes, in his book A Short History of the World, a record left by an official of the pharaoh about the view that the Egyptians had of the sovereign in this period: "He is a god to whom we owe life, father and mother of all men, unique and unparalleled".

With the decay of Egypt and the decline of the monarchy, the king's divine origin ended up being just a doctrine to legitimize whoever occupied the throne, even if it had a foreign origin, such as, for example, the Ptolemaic dynasty, of Macedonian origin.

The Social Classes

The Greek historian Herodotus described, in his work Histories, seven social classes in Egypt: priests, militaries, cattle breeders, pig breeders, merchants, interpreters and pilots (of boats). However, a more accurate and modern perspective distinguishes four classes: an upper class, which included the royal family, nobility, high officials, high priests, and generals; a middle class, with middle-level officials, priests, merchants, and farmers; a lower class, made up of artisans and free peasants; and finally, the slaves.

Due to the custom of Egyptian kings to keep several wives and a large number of concubines, an important part of the nobility was made up of the pharaoh's descendants and relatives.

Priests were the support of royal power. They were also the secret police and kept social order. By controlling the people's beliefs and benefiting from the pharaoh's dependence on their support, the priests became, over time, richer and more powerful than the aristocracy and, at certain points in Egypt's history, than the royal family. They educated young people, accumulated and transmitted

Priests offering birds to the gods, on a relief in the Temple of Medinet Habu, in Luxor, Egypt.

knowledge and tradition, and disciplined with zeal and rigor. The Greek historian Herodotus, described them in his book An Account of Egypt: "They are religious excessively beyond all other men, and with regard to this they have customs as follows [...]. They wear garments of linen always newly washed [...]. They circumcise themselves for the sake of cleanliness, preferring to be clean rather than comely. The priests shave themselves all over their body every other day, so that no lice or any other foul thing may come to be upon them when they minister to the gods [...]. These wash themselves in cold water twice in a day and twice again in the night". The high religious leaders knew the names of the gods, which were secret, as this knowledge allowed them to invoke the power of the deity. The clergy was sustained by resources paid by the subjects.

The tributes and taxes paid to the temples allowed the religious to own a third of all the land along the Nile.

A great part of the Egyptian population was made of peasants who provided labor for large public works and the surplus of their agricultural production, which sustained the noble classes, the bureaucracy and the large religious structure. The land was rich and cultivation techniques improved even more with enhancements in irrigation. Vegetables, barley and a type of wheat, emmer wheat,

The temple of Karnak and the sacred lake, residence of the gods Amun-Ra, his wife Mut and their son Khonsu.

Peasant with his cow, on a relief in the Temple of Luxor in Thebes, Egypt.

were the main crops and extended along the irrigation canals. The diet was supplemented with poultry, fish and game meat. Cattle were mainly used for traction and plowing. The greatest burden on the peasants was compulsory service in collective works. When they were not recruited by the pharaoh to carry out these activities, they enjoyed considerable leisure time.

Peasants were, initially, servants who worked on the monarch's properties or in the great temples. With the revolution that occurred in the First Intermediate Period, peasant families received land to cultivate by paying a tribute that constituted a part of the harvest. The lords of these lands were, however, the pharaoh, a temple, a nomarch or some landowner. In addition to working the land, peasants were recruited for military service and to work in public works. Slaves were, essentially, prisoners of war that the king gave to his soldiers as a reward for their military performance. However, slavery was not that important to the Egyptian economy. Slaves enjoyed certain legal protection and could be freed. It was also not uncommon for the poor to sell themselves as slaves to ensure food and housing for their family.

Feeding
The First Breads

The basis of the Egyptian feeding was bread. In fact, the oldest evidence of bread was found in Egypt. Although leavened bread probably must have existed in prehistoric times, the first archaeological finds of this product come from the country of the pharaohs. Breads were found in several tombs that were offered to the dead so that they could be fed on their journey to the Beyond, after physical death. Some of these breads were preserved for more than five thousand years due to the arid climate of that region.

These "mummified" breads allowed observations to be carried out with an electron microscope, which detected yeast cells in the dough. However, as breads in ancient Egypt were made with emmer wheat, this flour produced a hard crust, which impairs visual examination to determine whether all breads were really leavened. For this reason it is not known for sure how widespread the use of yeast was in Egypt during Antiquity – despite the certainty that it was used to a greater or lesser degree.

In the time of the pharaohs there were breads of several shapes, including those representing animals. The flour was made by grinding the grains in a pestle or a stone mill. It was unavoidable that small stones get mixed with the flour during the process. Many Egyptian mummies presented strong abrasion on their teeth as a result of chewing bread that contained sand and stones from mills and pestles.

Egyptian painting of food offering: meat, fruits, bread and wine.

Women

Egyptian women had, generally, more independence and a higher status than members of their gender in other civilizations. In fact, the freedom of the Egyptian women left Greek travelers, who confined their women, shocked. The Hellenes were astonished by noting that Egyptian women could publicly exert their activities without being bothered or persecuted. They could dispose of their assets and had guaranteed their legal rights.

Egyptian art depicts court ladies dressed in beautiful linen clothes, carefully combed and adorned with jewels, using special cosmetics, to which local merchants devoted great attention. Other evidence that attests the importance of women in Egyptian society are depictions of the pharaohs and their queens – as well as other noble couples –, portrayed with a correlation of feelings that suggests true emotional equality.

"They used all cosmetic resources, getting to paint their nails and eyes; some of them covered their necks, arms and ankles

Ancient Egyptian scroll.

with jewels", writes Will Durant in his book Heroes of History – A Brief History of Civilization from Ancient Times to the Dawn of the Modern Age. "They spoke of sex with a directness rivaling that of the freest women of today. They could take the initiative in courtship, and could be divorced only for proved adultery, or with ample compensation".

Beautiful women, like Nefertiti, wife of Akhenaten, depicted in many paintings and sculptures, reflect the power conquered by their gender, indicating political influence, non-existent in many other places. Many times, the power was passed down through the female lineage. An heiress conferred her husband the right of succession, which resulted in great concern with the marriage of princesses. Many royal marriages united brother and sister. Some pharaohs married their own daughters, sometimes more to avoid someone from marrying them than to preserve their divine blood. Some consorts exerted power and one of them, Hatshepsut, insisted on attending rituals with a false ceremonial beard, wearing men's clothing and bearing the title of pharaoh.

Statue of Queen Hatshepsut with the ceremonial beard worn by the pharaoh.

A woman carved in the ancient Egyptian necropolis of the nobles, in Thebes, Egypt.

There is also a great female presence in the Egyptian pantheon, notably in the cult of Isis. The literature and the pictorial arts emphasized respect for wives and mothers. Some women could read and write, and there is an Egyptian word to designate a scribe woman, although in fact there were not many occupations outside the home that were exerted by women, other than that of priestess or prostitute.

The Administration

In the lead of the different ministries there was a vizier, intermediary between the pharaoh and the government offices. The role of the vizier started right at the beginning of Egyptian civilization, consolidating itself in the sixth dynasty. The vizier acted as a magistrate, oversaw finance, public works, government archives, and customs.

After the sixth dynasty, the vizier's power came to be nominal, and his authority was only restored in the Middle Kingdom. At certain times there were two viziers, one responsible for Upper Egypt and the other for Lower Egypt.

Under the authority of the vizier was the administration of the provinces, the nomes. He was also responsible for the four major departments into which the administration of the Empire was divided. The first of these departments was the Treasury, which collected taxes and

The famous statue "The Seated Scribe", in the Louvre, Paris: one of the most important examples of Egyptian art.

ran the economy. The second was Agriculture, divided into a sector dedicated to livestock and other to agriculture. The third was the Royal Archive, which maintained property titles and civil records. The fourth department, Justice, was responsible for law enforcement.

In the New Kingdom, Egypt had an elaborate hierarchy of bureaucrats. In general, the most important people came from the nobility. Some of them were buried with a pomposity that rivaled that of the pharaoh. Less eminent families provided thousands of scribes to the staff of the government machine. These scribes, who had a prominent role in the administration of the Empire, were trained in a special school in Thebes. Their main characteristics can be known through texts that list the necessary skills to succeed as a scribe: dedication to studies, self-control, prudence, respect for superiors, extreme attention to the inviolability of weights and measures, mastery of legal rules.

The importance of the scribe, that is, his relevance in the administration of the Empire is portrayed in the famous stone statue, The Scribe, in the Louvre Museum. Seated on the floor in Oriental fashion, wearing only a white fabric petticoat, he has a "style", a reed pen behind his ear, as a spare for the one he is using. The papyrus rolls he handles probably record a list of work carried out and goods paid for, prices and costs, profits and losses, taxes receivable and payable, or contracts and wills he wrote. "His life is monotonous, but he consoles himself by writing essays on the hardships of the manual worker's existence and the princely dignity of those whose food is paper and whose blood is ink", writes Will Durant.

The Empire was divided into provinces, or nomes. There were 20 nomes in Lower Egypt and 22 in Upper Egypt. Their administration was carried out by nomarchs appointed by the pharaoh, but who sought to become hereditary lords. The scribes ran the empire under the supervision of the pharaoh, the clergy, and the nomarchs. Thus organized, the government charged taxes, accumulated capital, created a credit system, distributed resources to agriculture, industry, and commerce, and even developed a postal service.

The production of goods was carried out by free workers and slaves, under the orders of the nomarchs. Wars provided thousands of prisoners that were, for the most part, sold as slaves, whose labor made it easy mining and engineering triumphs.

Egyptian painting on the wall of the Temple of Ramesses II, in Abydos, showing tied up prisoners of war who will be sold as slaves.

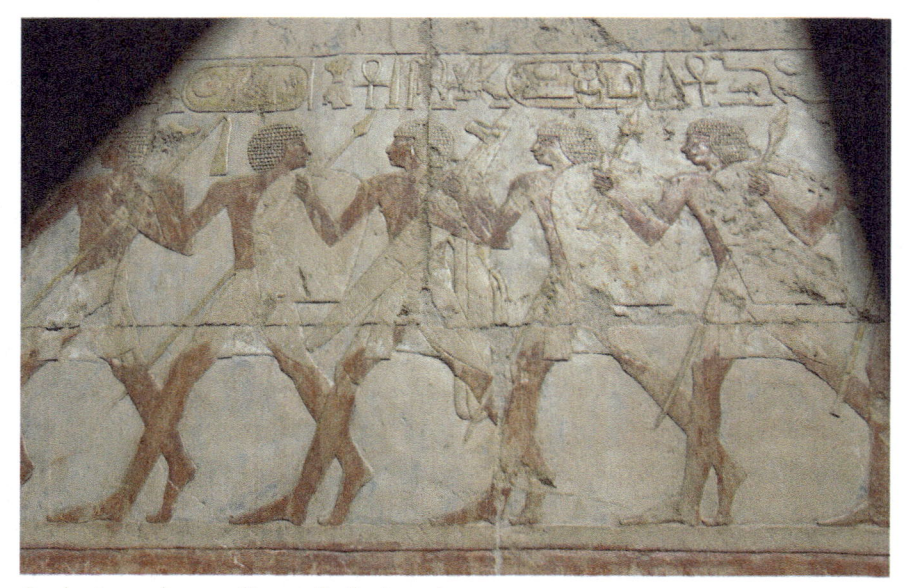

Ancient warriors on the wall of a temple.

Class conflicts were common. A papyrus records a claim of some workers to the supervisor: "We have been driven here by hunger and thirst; we have no clothes, no oil, no food. Write to our lord the Pharaoh, and to the governor who is over us, so that they may give us something for our sustenance" There was not, however, a class revolution – unless one considers the exodus of the Jews as such.

According to the American historian Will Durant, in ancient Egypt, the industrial arts were as advanced and varied as in medieval Europe. Egyptian artisans made bronze weapons and tools, saws and drilling instruments capable of cross hard stones such as diorite. They were masters at carving wood. They built merchant ships up to three hundred meters long and skiffs that are true artistic treasures.

The Army

In the Old Kingdom and at the beginning of the Middle Kingdom, Egypt did not dispose of a standing army. Each nome had its own militia, and the great temple properties, its police force. The Egyptian forces relied on a navy, which was limited to the Nile. There were In the Old Kingdom and at the beginning of the Middle Kingdom, Egypt did not dispose of a standing army. Each nome had its own militia, and the great temple properties, its police force. The Egyptian forces relied on a navy, which was limited to the Nile. There were numerous auxiliary forces, with Nubians, Libyans and Berbers. When there was a need, recruitment campaigns were carried out, and each village needed to contribute with a contingent of a certain size.

In the New Kingdom, the Army was better organized, and a corps of chariots drawn by two horses, carrying two men was created: a driver and a soldier. In the time of Ramesses II, the Army started being divided into four corps: Amun, Re, Ptah and Set. Each of them had five thousand men, grouped into twenty companies subdivided, in turn, into five groups of fifty men. The companies were led by professional officers and the groups, by officers of an equivalent level to sergeant. Two scribes managed the Army, one responsible for the troops and the other for provisions. Each company had its own scribe in charge of the organization.

Great Constructions

Until about 1800 BC, Egyptian engineering surpassed any other. Among its great deeds, it built canals connecting the Nile to the Red Sea and transported over long distances stones and obelisks that weighed thousands of tons, in addition to the colossal Pyramids of Giza.

From the left, the pyramids of the pharaohs Menkaure, Khafre and Khufu and those of the three queens (the smaller pyramids), in Giza, Egypt.

The houses and agricultural constructions were made of adobe and were not meant to challenge eternity. However, the palaces, tombs and memorials of the pharaohs were another matter – a matter of affirming the magnitude of Egyptian civilization and its king-god.

Under the guidance of a scribe, thousands of slaves and sometimes regiments of soldiers were deployed to manually cut and place in position huge ornate stone blocks, often carved and painted in an elaborate way. For that, they used, first, copper tools and, later, bronze. They did not dispose of cranes and pulleys, but used levers and mobile platforms, in addition to huge earth ramps, through which they lifted the stones to the top of the construction. In this way, the Egyptians produced monuments that, even today, surprise and intrigue due to their size and technical difficulty. Among their contributions to architecture are, in addition to the column, the arch, the vault, the capital, the architrave and the triangular pediment.

Because of the importance given to the construction of great monuments, by the example of Imhotep, the architects acquired great

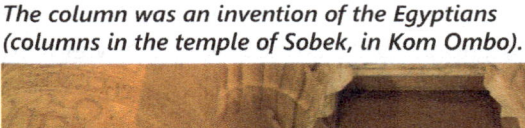

The column was an invention of the Egyptians (columns in the temple of Sobek, in Kom Ombo).

Pyramid of Meidum, in the shape of Mastaba.

prestige. More than riches and recognition, the constructors hoarded technical knowledge and developed technologies that made them legendary in a time when science meant magic. In fact, the constructions promoted by the clergy and the kings and carried out by the constructors resulted, especially with the development of writing, in an accumulation of culture that, according to J.M. Roberts, "became more and more effective as an instrument with which to change the world".

The most famous among the Egyptian monuments are the pyramids, which dominate the great complex of constructions intended to house the king after his death. Among the pyramids of the third dynasty, in Saqqara, near Memphis, it stands out the Step Pyramid, a masterpiece of the first known architect, Imhotep, vizier of the pharaoh, who is credited with the beginning of the construction in stone and who later would be deified as god of medicine and revered as astronomer, priest and wise. The construction of something unprecedented like this pyramid, just over sixty meters high, was certainly an event seen as proof of divine power.

The surplus of wealth enabled a succession of kings to build around 118 pyramids. As the land along the Nile was bordered only by escarpments and small mountains at the foot of larger ones, the pyramids achieved a domain that would be impossible in a mountainous landscape.

The first pyramids in Egypt were formed by steps, which were nothing more than stacked "mastabas". These mastabas, whose name derives from the Arabic maabba (stone bench), were tombs in the shape of a pyramid base built since the first dynastic era.

The first pyramid was built around 2700 BC and the largest pyramids were built in Giza, during the fourth dynasty. The pyramid of Cheops, also called the Great Pyramid, took twenty years to be completed, employing between five and six million tons of stone that were taken to the site from a distance of up to eight hundred kilometers. Designed to be 146 meters high, equivalent to a fifty-story building, it required the employment of approximately 100,000 workers, including slaves and farmers recruited when the floods were at their height, preventing them from working the land. This colossal construction is perfectly oriented, and its sides, about 230 meters long, vary less than twelve centimeters. It was the most impressive structure ever built in the world – especially because it was carried out in a kingdom where the population did not reach one million inhabitants.

However, despite their colossal size and the effort put in their construction, the pyramids did not represent a great advance in terms of

The Sphinx and the Pyramid of Khafre.

Temple of Kom Ombo.

architectural elaboration. The pyramids were not, however, the only great monuments erected by the ancient Egyptians. In other locations, there were great temples, palaces, and the tombs of the Valley of the Kings. Near the pyramid of the pharaoh Khafre (c. 2550 BC) is found one of the most intriguing monuments in history: the sphinx. Apparently by order of this ruler, his artists and artisans carved an imposing figure, symbol of his power, with the body of a lion and the head of Khafre himself. His face is gloomy, as if to frighten possible looters of the royal tomb.

Science

The monumental works carried out by the ancient Egyptians led these people to be considered as possessing great scientists, since these constructions would require the most refined mathematical and scientific knowledge. However, although Egyptian surveying was highly skilled and the civil servants of the Empire were perfect civil engineers, elementary mathematics was enough to erect the monuments they built. It was enough competence in measuring and knowledge of a few formulas to calculate volume and weight. "The Egyptians did not rival Babylon in the sciences," writes J.M. Roberts. Their "one solid achievement was the calendar", states the author.

Other authors disagree, pointing to advances in other areas. "In medicine, the Egyptians probably led the world then," writes Geoffrey Blainey, author of A Brief History of the World. The magic and practical knowledge of medicine and drugs were merged. Good part of the knowledge of the human body came from the practice of mummification, when the corpse and its internal organs were handled. The Egyptians developed efficient methods in orthopedics, surgery, pharmacy and possibly were the first to use bandages and splints. There is evidence that trepanations they performed to relieve cranial pressure resulting from trauma were successful. "In their cures, they used the fat of creatures like rats and snakes, herbs and vegetables, carefully weighing and measuring each ingredient," attests Blainey. According to Homer, in The Odyssey, the Egyptian physicians were the best of their time.

The Egyptian Calendar

A great contribution of the Egyptians was the introduction of their calendar. The development of the calendar came from the need for the first civilizations to measure time periods because of agriculture, reli-

The Egyptian calendar on an original papyrus.

gion, business or to determine their chronology. The first calendar to meet these needs was the Egyptian one, which was later perfected by the Romans in the Julian calendar, used in Europe for over 1500 years.

The ancient Egyptians used a lunar calendar and synchronized it with a sidereal calendar. For this, they observed the seasonal appearance of the star Sirius, which they called Sopdet. This cycle corresponds to the solar year, being only twelve minutes shorter. To synchronize the two calendars, the Egyptians adopted a civil year of 360 days divided into three seasons with four months of 30 days and interspersed five days throughout this year. This civil calendar was used to administrative and governmental purposes, while the lunar calendar continued to regulate everyday matters and religion. But because of the discrepancy between these calendars, which lost synchrony by one day every four years, the Egyptians established a second lunar calendar based on the civil year, instead of observing the star Sopdet, with the intercalation of a month every time the first day of the lunar year fell before the first day of the calendar year. This calendar was used to determine religious festivals. The other lunar calendar was kept and applied to agriculture. Thus, the Egyptians started using three different calendars, each one with a specific purpose. The only unit greater than the year was the reign of a pharaoh. Like the Babylonians, the Egyptians also used regal years to denominate a period, stipulating its chronology as "year one, two, etc..., of the Pharaoh Necho II", for example. With each new regent, the count went back to year one.

The civil year was divided into three seasons: Flood or Inundation, when the Nile River overflowed over farmland; Emergence, when the Nile returned to its bed and planting had started; and Low Water, season when the waters were low and it was harvest time. The months were numbered according to the season to which they belonged, "second month of the Inundation", for example. The day was counted from sunrise and was divided into unequal hours that varied according to the time of year. They used clepsydras (water clocks) and sundials to mark them.

An Exceptional Civilization

Despite the colossal deeds and the long lasting of the Egyptian empire, this civilization did not develop the impressive resources created in the early times. The Egyptians were capable of gathering colossal resources of labor and material, under the guidance of civil servants, but only to build the greatest tombs that History has already recorded. In the same way, their refined art was used almost exclusively to adorn monuments. Their elite, highly educated, using complex writing and having in the papyrus a cheap material with great power to disseminate information, which they used to record bureaucratic texts and inscriptions, did not bequeath to humanity any great philosophical ideas. Even the military and economic power of Egypt had little influence on the world in a permanent way; neither their civilization expanded overseas. Unlike the Greeks – who left their marks, establishing a cultural legacy that became the root of Western civilization –, the Egyptians did not influence other people so much, or constitute an inheritance that became the basis of another civilization.

Despite this, the staying capacity of Egyptian civilization is astonishing – probably the greatest deed of this people. It existed for a long time, suffering two eclipse phases, from which it recovered. This long stay represents great success – a success that few civilizations conquered.

The Sphinx and the pyramid: eternal symbols of Egypt.

The Dynasties

Protodynastic Period
After the people who would become the Egyptians settled along the Nile, they founded colonies that fought against each other. Over time, they formed two kingdoms, the North and the South. During this period, the entire basis of Egyptian culture was established – religion, funerary rites and writing, which would gradually develop in the hieroglyphs.

Ancient Egyptian hieroglyphs as symbols of Earth's history.

Egyptian village in the oasis of Siwa.

In fact, there is more information about primitive Egyptian civilization than any other at such a remote date. From the earliest times, the Egyptians had a form of pictographic writing, that is, it used drawings of objects, animals, etc., to represent an idea. Over time, these pictograms started representing sounds and developed the hieroglyphs. As it was difficult to write, hieroglyphic writing did not spread beyond Egypt, although its use had been prolonged. The last known example of this writing dates from the 5th century AD. From then on, its domain was lost until its key was deciphered, at the beginning of the 19th century, with the discovery of the famous Rosetta Stone. This stele is written in Demotic Greek (an Egyptian language that appeared at a late stage) and with hieroglyphs, which allowed its translation, opening the way to the knowledge of ancient Egypt, due to the large number of inscriptions in tombs, monuments and papyri that survived until our time.

Some of the last kings of the predynastic period left monuments. The most famous of them, although little is known about him, was The Scorpion King, a pharaoh who promoted wars and paved the way for the unification of the two kingdoms.

The Old Kingdom (2700 to 2200 BC)

According to the first narratives recorded in hieroglyphs, around 3000 BC, Egypt was already divided into two empires: Lower and Upper Egypt. Accounts refer to a southern king named Menes who conquered the north and established his dynasty. This first Egyptian dynasty was known as "Thinite" because its members came from the village of Thinis.

According to this tradition, Menes, the founder of the city of Memphis, reigned in unified Egypt between 3150 – 3125 BC. The territory under his control extended for approximately one thousand kilometers along the Nile. It is not known for sure what this government meant, but as noted in his book A Short History of the World, British historian J.M. Roberts, "What its government meant is hard to say, but it is an impressive achievement to have established even a claim to rule so big an area". Menes gave rise to a period of about two thousand years, during which Egypt was, in general, under a single ruler, a single religious system, and a pattern of government and society, without the interference of outside influence. Although there have been ups and downs in this period, this continuity is surprising. This is what made great achievements possible, whose traces still fascinate and excite our imagination.

The crown of the Empire: the red deshret, from Lower Egypt, united to the white hedjet, from Upper Egypt.

An important contribution occurred during the first dynasty was the invention of sheets of paper made from papyrus, which allowed the preservation of a great part of Egypt's artistic and cultural production. The papyrus grew in the swamps of the Nile. In about 2700 BC, the Egyptians turned the papyrus into a thick type of paper, similar to the scroll, ready to receive the pen marks, or "style," of reed. Made with bundles of overlapping papyrus, arranged criss-crossed and crumpled until they form a homogeneous sheet, this invention made a great advance possible for humanity, as it allowed the multiplication of the recording of information. In fact, paper did more for communication than hieroglyphs. Papyrus was cheaper than the skin from which scrolls were made, and easier to write on, handle, and store than clay tablets and stone plates. Shortly after the appearance of the papyrus, the scribes started pasting sheets together to form a long roll. In this way, the Egyptians invented both the book and the material on which the first of them would be written. Great part of what is known about ancient Egypt came to us through the papyrus.

The Thinite kings, descendants of Menes, about whom little is known, also founded the second Egyptian dynasty. The Thinites sought to consolidate the union of the country and defend its borders.

From that time on, the king came to be seen as an incarnation of Horus, the falcon god, and protected by two goddesses: Nekbet, from

Sheet of paper made from papyrus.

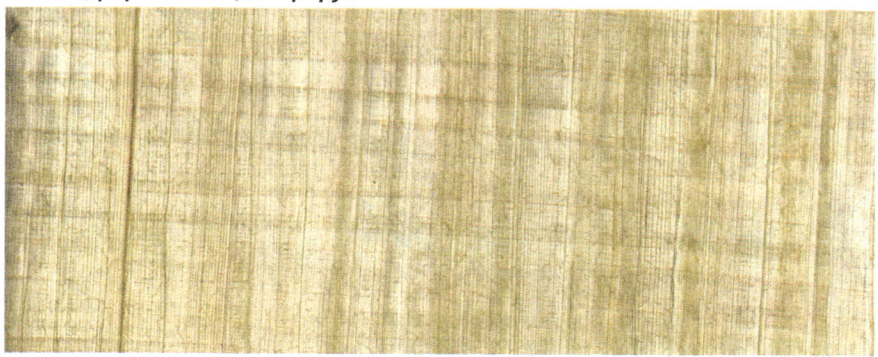

Mastaba M17, in Meidum, Egypt.

Upper Egypt, incarnated in a raven, and Buto, from Lower Egypt, who assumed the form of a snake. The king's greatest symbol was the double crown: the white one, from Upper Egypt, and the red one, from Lower Egypt.

The Thinite dynasties also implemented the type of civil, military, and priestly organization that were characteristic of Egyptian civilization. The king was advised by a vizier and by the administrators of the regions of the Empire, who supervised the collection of taxes, the construction of irrigation works and tombs, and the mastabas, which will originate the future pyramids. The Army was composed of soldiers supplied by the villages, under the supreme command of the king and under the orders of the chiefs of the fortresses. The priestly class had also started establishing itself under Menes, with different groups of priests, such as the Zematis, presiding over several cults.

It was under the kings of the Thinite second dynasty that the first mastabas, the funerary monuments that preceded the pyramids, were built.

The third dynasty has its central figure in King Djoser (c. 2700 BC), famous for his wisdom and good government. His vizier, the architect Imhotep, built the first stone pyramid, in Saqqara. An important development took place under the kings of this dynasty. In the second millennium before Christ, the knowledge accumulated by navigators and shipbuilders about wind regimes and sea currents was already used and, in about 2650 BC, the Egyptians of the third dynasty used, for the first time, the square sail, probably made of leather, in ships on the high seas.

The Pyramid of Khafre in Giza, Egypt.

The fourth dynasty marks the classical period of the Old Kingdom. During this period, the power was centralized in the hands of the pharaoh. It is at this time that the great pyramid constructors lived: Khufu (Cheops), Khafre and Menkaure (Mycerinus). The construction of these colossal monuments, which required the mobilization of a huge labor force, compromised productive activities, and the country impoverished.

The fifth dynasty (2500 – 2350 BC) continued constructing pyramids, although on a smaller scale. Relations with neighbors were encouraged, and military and commercial expeditions were sent to Syria and Nubia. The oldest narrative about a sea crossing is from this time. Ordered by the pharaoh Sneferu, sovereign of Egypt from approximately 2575 to 2551 BC, the fleet of 40 ships sailed to the port of Byblos, a Phoenician port city of Gebal, and returned loaded with noble woods. However, Sneferu did not become famous for encouraging sea travels, as his subjects were not enthusiastic sailors, but for the pyramid he erected. The Egyptians were more concerned with preparing for the afterlife than taking advantage of their geographical location, which was conducive to the development of navigation. The lack of suitable wood for the construction of ships in that country may have been a factor holding back the progress of nautical arts. In addition, it was easier to travel the River Nile than to navigate the Egyptian coast. It would take nearly a thousand years so that the pharaoh Sesostris awoke the interest of the Egyptians in exploring the sea.

At the end of the fifth dynasty started a trend that was consolidated in the sixth dynasty (2350 – 2200 BC), in which power was slowly passing to the governors of the provinces, the nomarchs.

First Intermediate Period (2200 – 2050 BC

The First Intermediate Period witnessed an inversion of the previous trend. In this way, Egypt was invaded, and people of Asiatic origin settled for a time in the lower valley of the Nile.

Almost nothing is known about the seventh and eighth dynasties, as the nomes were completely autonomous.

The founder of the ninth dynasty, Khety I, made culture flourish again and established a center of power centered in Herakleopolis, the city where he reigned. Other centers of local power were formed, with Thebes at the forefront. Soon a dispute started for the domain of Egypt. It was only the 12th dynasty that re-established control over Upper and Lower Egypt, under Amenemhet I, a member of a family of high officials of the Theban kings.

The Middle Kingdom (2050 – 1800 BC)

The Middle Kingdom was inaugurated by a powerful king, Amenemhet I, who reunified the kingdom from his capital in Thebes.

Although the nomes continued to have great independence, Egypt increased its sphere of power under the 12th dynasty.

Egyptian stamp from 1993 with effigy of the pharaoh Amenemhet III.

The pharaohs of this dynasty adopted aggressive expansion policies. Their ships filled the port of Byblos, in Gebal (today, Lebanon), where they carried out active trade. The sea also took them to Crete and the Red Sea, where they expanded their influence. Palestine was controlled by Egypt, which sent military expeditions to Libya and Nubia.

For nearly 250 years, Egypt went through a period of recovery, especially in terms of order and social cohesion. There was, equally, a material development. Great works of recovery were carried out on the Nile swamps. To the south, the pharaohs of the 12th dynasty conquered Nubia, expanding their territory. During this period, the pharaoh's divine condition subtly changed. He was not just a god, but a descendant of the gods.

However, although the descendants of Amenemhet I had ensured more than two centuries of prosperity to Egypt, under the

The temple of Luxor in Thebes, capital of the pharaohs of the 12th dynasty.

13th dynasty although also Theban, divisionism reappeared, and the Middle Kingdom ended amidst political disturbances and dynastic competitions.

Second Intermediate Period (1800 – 1550 BC)

During the 14th dynasty, the kings were elected for short periods and the power was not hereditary but controlled by the viziers. The Second Intermediate Period, which lasted approximately two hundred years, was marked by another incursion of foreigners, the Hyksos. From 1730 BC, the Hyksos, a Semitic people who started occupying the eastern region of Nile Delta from the 12th dynasty, gradually assumed power. The Hyksos, or "shepherd kings", disposed of their enemies due to their better military technology: chariots with horses, compound bows, bronze weapons and advanced techniques for the construction of fortifications. The Hyksos completed the conquest of Egypt in 1675 BC and, in the following year, founded the 15th dynasty.

Apparently, the invaders adopted Egyptian conventions and methods, even keeping, in a first moment, the existing bureaucrats.

One of the rulers of this period, Sesostris IV, who lived around 1650 BC, was the first pharaoh who strove to overcome the Egyptians' lack of interest in the sea. He sent expeditions in trade travels as well as exploration journeys, in order to conceive a geographical concept of his territory. It is not known, however, what was the extent of his discoveries. Sesostris realized the need to build a solid navy and created among his subjects the class of sailors, which stimulated a greater proximity between the sea and the Egyptians, oceanophobes by tradition.

Ancient historians, such as the Greek Herodotus (484-424 BC), considered the Father of History, state that Sesostris ordered the founding of an Egyptian colony in a place called Phasis, where ships were built, maps were designed, and nautical sciences were developed. During the reign of Sesostris, the Egyptians came to dominate

Egyptian war chariot.

the trade on the Red Sea and found colonies and warehouses in Greece. But Sesostris ruled in a period when his country was facing a series of disturbances and, with his death, the Egyptians returned to their natural disinterest in the sea. The overseas colonies lost contact with the metropole and, as before the pharaoh, trade was once again dominated by foreigners.

The Liberation War

The Hyksos also founded the 16th dynasty. Under their domain, around 1650 BC, a new independent Theban dynasty emerged – the 17th–, which would enthrone fifteen pharaohs. The Theban monarchs maintained good relations with the Hyksos, but Tao I (it is believed he reigned only one year, between 1550 and 1549 BC) started the conflict with the Hyksos, which, after his death, was continued by his successors. Ahmose, a descendant of Tao, founded the 18th dynasty around 1570 BC and completed the expulsion of the Hyksos, who had taken refuge in Palestine. The reign of Ahmose's son, Amenhotep I (reigned between about 1526 and 1506 BC), marks the beginning of the formation of the New Kingdom of Egypt.

The New Kingdom

The period known as the New Kingdom was, at its apogee, very successful in terms of international influence and left elaborate monuments as a testimony of the development of this time. During the 18th dynasty, there was a renaissance of the arts, a transformation of military techniques due to the adoption of tactics and equipment from people of the Middle East and Asia, such as the war chariot. This was all possible because of the strong consolidation of royal authority.

Monuments recording the arrival of tributes and slaves, as well as marriages to Asian princesses testify Egyptian sovereignty.

The reign of Amenhotep I lasted about twenty years. Childless, he left the throne of Egypt to his sister, Ahmose. However, according to Egyptian custom, it was her husband, Thutmose I, who became pharaoh. He needed to suppress a Nubian rebellion and promoted a cam-

Reliefs on the walls of the Temple of Karnak celebrate Egyptian victories in war.

Temple of Hatshepsut, near Luxor.

paign in Syria, reaching as far as the Upper Euphrates. Under his regency, the Egyptian empire reached the maximum of its expansion. Only one daughter of Thutmose I and Ahmose survived, princess Hatshepsut. When the pharaoh died, the throne passed to the pharaoh's eldest son with another princess, Thutmose II. To ensure the legitimacy of the succession, the new pharaoh married his half-sister Hatshepsut. Despite having fragile health, the reign of Thutmose II was a positive period for Egypt. Crowned at the age of twenty, he needed to amass and send a powerful army against the Nubians, which killed all the men of that nation. As Thutmose II and Hatshepsut did not have a son, the pharaoh named his son with a secondary wife, Thutmose III, to replace him. However, when Thutmose II died in about 1490 BC, Thutmose III was too young to rule, and Hatshepsut took the throne until the heir was old enough to head the Empire. Hatshepsut was the first queen to rule Egypt. However, when Thutmose III came of age, in 1486 BC, Hatshepsut assumed royal power, with the support of her adviser, architect and probable lover, Senenmut, reigning until 1468 BC.

The First Female Pharaoh

Hatshepsut's reign (circa 1503 to 1480 BC) contrasted with the warlike tendencies of the dynasty preceding hers, as she devoted herself to strengthening trade, to restore ancient monuments, and the construction of new ones. Entrepreneurial, in her twenty-three years of government, she left more works than any other Egyptian queen who succeeded her. As the first woman to sit on the throne of Horus, the falcon god that the pharaoh embodied, she had many obstacles to overcome and used all her political skill to do so. In public appearances and artistic depictions, she was characterized as a king, with a false beard and wearing the khepresh, a helmet used exclusively by the pharaohs on the battlefield. One of her maneuvers to legitimize the right to the throne was the construction of the temple of Deir el Bahari, or "northern convent", in Thebes, one of the great legacies of ancient Egypt. Designed by Senenmut, who, in addition to being an innovative architect, was the queen's lover, the temple dedicated to the gods Amun and Hathor records the most notable event of Hatshepsut's reign. Decorating an important wing of Deir el-Bahari there are a series of reliefs that describe in detail the expedition that Hatshepsut sent to the Land of Punt.

The Expedition to the Land of Punt

The bas-reliefs tell that Amun himself, the main god of Thebes, inspired the queen to order the journey to Punt, in present-day Somalia, a region rich in gums, resins, aromatic woods, amber, gold, lapis lazuli, and ivory. These products were traded in Egypt, Mesopotamia, Syria and Asia Minor exclusively by the Arabs. The god Amun, according to his protégé, intended to end the depen-

Relief in the Temple of Deir el-Bahari.

dency that his priests had on these merchants to obtain the oils and incense needed to carry out their elaborate rituals. For this reason, he ordered Hatshepsut to undertake the expedition. The queen, in turn, ordered the construction of five ships, the largest ever made in Egypt until then. They measured about 70 feet and had a very high stern and bow, with balustrades that served as an observatory and where there should be some kind of shelter for the officers. The ships had no decks and there was only one mast, made of a massive palm tree trunk, about nine meters high. The crew consisted of thirty oarsmen, fifteen on each side, four sailors, two helmsmen, a first mate and a captain. A military detachment also accompanied the expedition, it was the honor guard of Hatshepsut's ambassador. In total, it is presumed that around 210 people have participated in the expedition on the five ships

Unfortunately, many inscriptions and paintings of the temple are mutilated, breaking the continuity of the narration. Even so, the set tells minute details and allows one to have a very clear idea of that trip.

Relief painted on the temple of Hatshepsut, with rural workers.

Warriors who accompanied the expedition to Punt (decoration of the temple of Hatshepsut).

It is assumed that the expedition had sailed from Thebes and reached the Red Sea by some ancient river course that connected the river to the sea. If such a passage really existed, it disappeared in the following centuries, since other pharaohs strove to dig a canal connecting the Nile to the Red Sea. The reliefs make no reference to the travel by sea and the narration continues with the arrival of the flotilla in Punt, where it was received by the prince of the place, named Parihu, and his wife. Ati, the princess, is depicted as extremely fat, almost misshapen. So much that some scholars raised the possibility that she had suffered from elephantiasis. However, it is more likely that all this weight was just the standard of beauty imposed upon women in certain parts of Africa, where the ideal was that beauties, fattened on a base of banana beer, to become so obese that they could barely walk.

After landing, Hatshepsut's ambassador gifted Parihu regally and received in return the precious goods from Punt, which included, among other curious rarities, an elephant and a giraffe. Then the Egyptian ambassador hosted a reception for Parihu, Ati and their court. An inscription below this depiction, on the mural of the temple of Deir el-Bahari, informs the feast menu: "bread, beer, wines, meat, vegetables and all the good things from Egypt, by order and will of His Majesty, our Life, Health and Strength".

The walls of the temple of Amun and Hathor tell nothing about the return trip, but attest to the arrival of the ships in Thebes loaded with treasures. The depiction is so faithful that modern ichthyologists were able to identify specimens of Somali fish among the fauna brought from Punt. The drawings describe the huge welcoming procession that accompanied the explorers, escorted by a detachment of the Army's elite, through the streets of Thebes to the Deir el-Bahari, where the queen was waiting for them. The paintings conclude their story by saying that Hatshepsut received the travelers in triumph, in the presence of Hathor herself, the ruling goddess of the Land of Punt.

In addition to these fragments of memory echoing in the empty corridors of Deir el-Bahari, not much is known. Information is lacking to explain whether the expedition established a regular trade route with Punt, or whether it was a political maneuver by the astute Hatshepsut, a glorious adventure that inflated the ego and won the trust of her subjects.

Detail of the statue of Hatshepsut with the false beard of the pharaohs, in her temple, in Deir el-Bahari.

In 1468 BC, when Thutmose III was about thirty years old, he managed to overthrow the usurpers from power. In about 1480 BC, the queen's name disappeared from the monuments. It may be that she has simply resigned in favor of Thutmose III, which is unlikely. Apparently, through her successor's vengeful effort to erase Hatshepsut's name from all public records and statues, she remained on the throne until the end. Thutmose III did not even spare her mummy, which appears to have been destroyed. In 1881, the remains of Thutmose I, II and III were discovered in the tomb of the Priest Kings near Deir el-Bahari. In the mausoleum, nothing of Hatshepsut was found, except for an ivory-coated wooden cabinet, engraved with the queen's name. Inside it there was a dissected human liver. It is possible that the organ belonged to Hatshepsut herself.

But, despite the apparent cruelty, to the point, maybe, of destroying the mummy of his predecessor, thus denying her the eternity, Thutmose III was a great king. He had extraordinary political and military talent, expanding Egyptian territory. He went down in history as one of Egypt's greatest sovereigns.

However, Thutmose III ruled in a different scenario than his predecessors. By the end of the New Kingdom, the world outside Egypt had changed. External pressures increased, with the development of new military powers. Proof of this is that Thutmose III took seventeen years to dominate the territories to the east, having to give up expansion, held by a people called Mitanni, who dominated eastern Syria and northern Mesopotamia.

Akhenaten

Egypt reached its apogee in terms of prestige and prosperity with the pharaoh Amenhotep III (c. 1410 – 1375 BC). It was the greatest age of Thebes, and, as if to mark this fact, the pharaoh was buried in the greatest tomb ever erected for a king. Unfortunately, nothing remains of this funerary monument, except fragments of huge statues that the Greeks came to call the Colossi of Memnon, in reference to the legendary hero of Ethiopian origin.

Thutmose III defeating enemies, in relief in the Temple of Karnak, Luxor.

His successor, Amenhotep IV, had his education strongly influenced by the priests of Heliopolis, for whom the sun-god Re Harakhty was the greatest of all gods. Amenhotep IV cared more about art than war. A poet, he wrote the most famous poem in Egyptian literature and devoted himself to loving his wife, the beautiful Nefertiti, with whom he was portrayed driving his chariot or playing with his daughters. The ancient chronicles tell that, on ceremonial occasions, Nefertiti sat by his side and held his hand, while the daughters had fun at the foot of the throne. The queen bore him seven daughters, but no son. Even so, Amenhotep IV loved her so much that he did not take a second wife. He even expressed his love in public life. As an oath, the pharaoh adopted the phrase "just as my heart rejoices with the queen and her daughters".

Amenhotep IV also had a great devotion to the Sun, one of the main gods of the ancient Egyptians, venerated as the father of all earthly life. After his crowning, Amenhotep IV proclaimed himself the first priest of Re-Harakhty. In the fourth year of his reign, the pharaoh decided to construct, in Amarna, a new city dedicated to the sun-god, which would be called Akhetaten. The city was constructed quickly, and the king moved there in the sixth year of his regency. Right after moving to the new capital, Amenhotep made Aten – the solar disk – official as the god of the state religion and, to mark his sincerity, changed his name to Akhenaten, which means "the one who is favorable to Aten". Akhenaten not only made the cult of the sun-god mandatory, but also prohibited other religious manifestations.

However, the opposition caused by Akhenaten's religious revolution served to limit his power. The official hierarchy raged and conspired against the pharaoh. The people, encouraged by the priests, considered Akhenaten's monotheism a heresy, a severe offense against the gods, and rebelled. Even in the palace, Akhenaten was frowned upon, not only for religious reform, but for despising war and for having weakened the army. Because of this, the subject states refused to pay the due tributes and, one by one, deposed the Egyptian governors and freed themselves. Furthermore, the Hittites – a warlike people who established a mighty empire in Anatolia, present day Turkey – were putting pressure on Egyptian possessions. Akhenaten was unable to save

Bust of Nefertiti in the Egyptian Museum in Berlin.

Egyptian papyrus showing that the rays of Aten touch things, giving life to everything.

the Mitannis which, by that point, had allied with the Egyptians. With no support from the Egyptians, the Mitannis were deprived of all their lands west of the Euphrates.

Akhenaten lost almost all the support he had – only his wife and a few allies stayed by his side. He was just over thirty when he died. Two years after his death, he was succeeded by his son-in-law Tutankhaten. The new pharaoh, who later changed his name to Tutankhamun, was only nine years old when he acceded to the throne. Who held, in fact, the power was the old vizier, Ay. The change of the king's name marked the restoration of the ancient cult and demonstrated the end of the attempted religious reform. The pharaoh died young, aged about nineteen. Probably, the magnificent burial of Tutankhamun, in the Valley of the Kings, shows the gratitude of the priests for the return to the old religious order.

In the succession dispute that took place after his death, Horemheb, who since the reign of Akhenaten had been commander of the Army, took the throne. Horemheb reigned for thirty years, completely eliminating the vestiges of Aten's religion. With no descendants, he chose Ramesses as his successor.

The Dynasties

Another view of the Temple of Karnak, in Luxor, Egypt.

The sun-god receiving offerings.

The Ramessides

Ramesses I was already elderly when he took over the kingdom in 1319 BC. He died a year later and passed on the crown to his son, Seti I (1318 – 1301 BC), who undertook military campaigns, restoring the territory lost by Akhenaten. The twentieth dynasty was founded by the pharaoh Setnakhte (1197 – 1195 BC), and continued until 1157 BC, with Ramesses IV.

In addition to the traditional antagonists, new enemies appeared. The people of the Aegean Sea, or People of the Sea, were in full expansion. According to Egyptian records, the Aegean islands "go beyond their people", and "no land prevented them from advancing". The so-called "people of the sea" were eventually defeated, but it was an arduous effort.

Detail of the death mask of Tutankhamun.

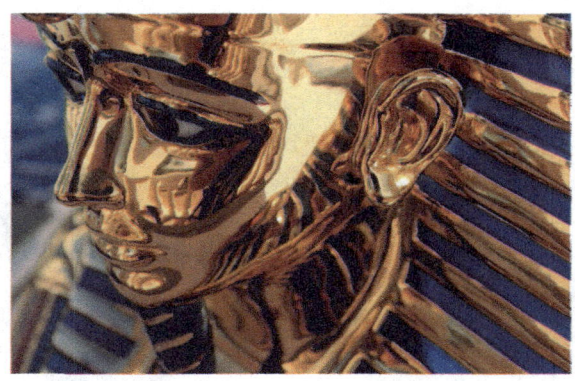

Ramesses II, who ruled Egypt from 1279 to 1213 BC, established a new age of prosperity and glory. His reign was one of the periods of greatest economic, administrative, military and cultural development. Ramesses II reconquered the Egyptian colonies, erected huge temples, and fathered a hundred sons and fifty daughters in his many wives. Around 1150 BC, increased the level of evidence of internal disorganization. Ramesses III was murdered as a result of a conspiracy in his harem. From then on, economic problems multiplied.

CIndeed, the Ramessides, as the pharaohs from Ramesses IV to Ramesses XI (1116–1090) are known, mark a period of decay. Although

Statue of Ramesses II in the Temple of Luxor.

Colossal statues of Ramesses II wearing the double crown of Lower and Upper Egypt.

they had kept Nubia, they lost control of Syria and Palestine to the Assyrians, while the Hebrews laid hold Canaanite cities. Among the main deeds of the Ramesside pharaohs are the extraordinary funerary monuments they constructed in the Valley of the Kings.

With the decrease of resources, the king's authority weakened. Effective power was, in fact, in the hands of the Army. The priests of Amun also took advantage of the situation, accumulating power and wealth. The oracle of the Imperial Temple of Karnak communicated the will of Amun, competing with the pharaoh's divine authority. The sacred nature of the kings was also challenged by tomb raiders, eager to seize the treasures buried with the sovereigns. During this period, the mummies of the great pharaohs had to be removed from their mausoleums to be hidden in the cliffs near the temple of Deir el Bahari. Ramesses XI was only an apparent monarch, while Smendes, monarch of Tanis, held effective power along with Herihor. When Ramesses XI died in 1090 BC, Smendes founded the 21st dynasty by proclaiming himself pharaoh, by marrying the daughter of Ramesses XI, to legitimize his position.

At the end of the second millennium before Christ, the decay that Egypt was going through at the end of the New Kingdom also occurred with other kingdoms, such as the Hittites. At that time, as noted by historian J.M. Roberts in his A Short History of the World, "it was dying the world that served as a scenario for the Egyptian glories". This decline of older civilizations certainly dragged Egypt in its wake.

Third Intermediate Period

The 21st dynasty (1070 – 945 BC) was marked by a division of power between the pharaoh, in Tanis, and the high priest of Amun, in Karnak and Thebes. It was also a period of decay and Egypt failed to maintain its domain in Syria, Palestine and Nubia. The Libyans, descendants of former prisoners of war, conquered an increasing power in Bubastis, in Lower Egypt, between Memphis and Tanis. When Psusennes, the last monarch of the 21st dynasty, died without heirs, in 945 BC, Shoshenq (or, according to the Bible, Shishak), a warlord from Bubastis, descen-

Interior of the temple in Abu Simbel.

dent of Libyans, ascended to the throne, inaugurating the 22nd dynasty. Shoshenq ruled vigorously, renewing the Egyptian presence in Palestine and Nubia, but his successors failed to maintain Egypt's unity. The Nubians advanced to the south, taking cities and territories. In 715 BC, the Nubian prince Shabaka established himself in Memphis as pharaoh.

The successors of Shabaka, however, had to face the Assyrians and were defeated in the wars they fought. The Assyrians dethroned the Nubian pharaoh Taharqa (690 – 664 BC) and imposed to Egypt a vassal king, Necho I (672 BC). Taharka's nephew, Tantamani, managed to recover Egypt and execute Necho, but the Assyrians attacked again in 663 BC, expelling Tantamani, taking Thebes and founding the Saite dynasty.

The Last Centuries

Under the Saite dynasty, Egypt rose again under the command of the princes of the city of Sais, in the Nile Delta, expelling the invader. During this period, known as the Saite Renaissance (663 – 525 BC), the country breathed a breath of freedom for the last time, before being conquered successively by the Persians (525 BC), the Greeks (332 BC)

Necho II sought to conquer naval power for the Egyptians.

and the Romans (30 BC). It was in this brief period of relative tranquility that the last great Egyptian expedition took place, and which was, if it was really successful, one of the most audacious sea crossings ever recorded. Ordered by the pharaoh Necho II, who reigned between 610 and 595 BC, and manned by Phoenician navigators, the expedition had the ambitious mission of circumnavigating Africa.

Necho II was a pharaoh who tried to respond boldly to the changes taking place in his time. To defend his territory, he supported an old enemy – the weakened Assyrians – against the growing Babylonian threat, but, after having achieved significant victories, he ended up defeated by Nebuchadnezzar. Equally bold was his response to the expansion of trade in the Nile Delta. To encourage this growth, Necho II started digging a canal that would connect the Nile to the Red Sea. After years of work and the death of 120,000 Egyptian workers, the pharaoh gave up on the construction of the canal, advised by an oracle who predicted that the work would only benefit the barbarians. Therefore, the restless Necho II, set up an expedition with the mission of circumnavigating Africa. To this end, he hired Phoenician sailors and ordered them to sail along the African coast, from the Red Sea, returning by the Pillars of Hercules, to the north, thus circumventing the continent. Herodotus, the Greek historian who told of the feat, reported that the explorers headed straight for Ethiopia, where they landed to plant cereals and replenish supplies, leaving after the harvest. In this way, they traveled for two years, always stopping to plant and get provisions. In the third year, they finally passed the Pillars of Hercules, the old name for the Strait of Gibraltar, and arrived back in Egypt.

Herodotus was a conscious investigator, as it is assumed in the name of his book, Istorie, or Investigation, which originated the term History, the science that Herodotus helped to create. He certainly checked the facts he told, even having written about the circumnavigation of Africa more than a century after Necho II. But, in fact, there are strong arguments that testify against the possibility of success of the expedition. The Journey time, for example, was too short. It is also considered that

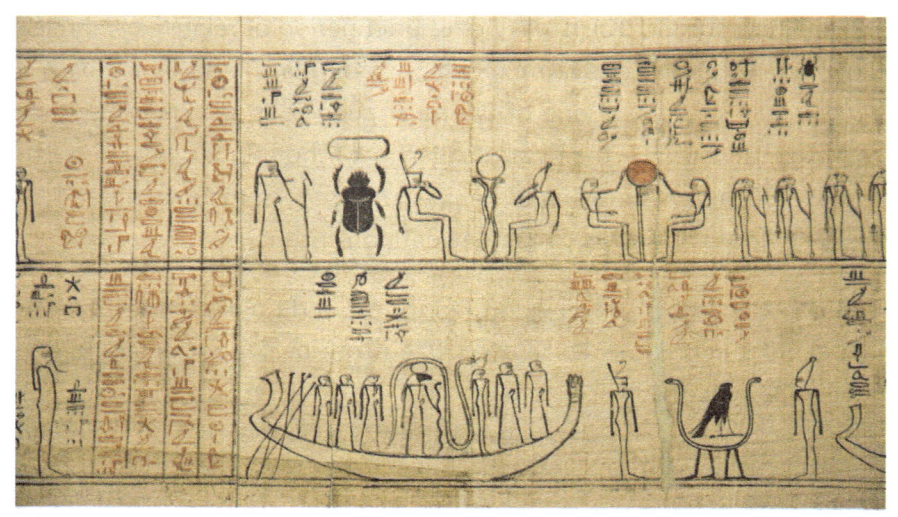

Fragment of papyrus containing travel narrative.

the ships of that time were not strong enough to complete the route in all its extension, nor did the sailors have enough knowledge and skills to conquer their intention. Two thousand years after Necho II, with much more advanced nautical technology and after many attempts, the Portuguese circumvented the cape in the extreme south of Africa, which they called Cape of Storms and then renamed it to Cape of Good Hope. The titanic Portuguese effort to circumnavigate Africa, mythically sung by Camões in "The Lusiads", pales any argument that the expedition of Necho II was really successful and would be enough to put an end to this discussion.

However, there are two consistent pieces of evidence that the African continent was circumnavigated in Antiquity. Herodotus wrote that the Phoenician sailors of Necho "reported that when they circumvented Libya (the name by which the Greeks called Africa) they had the sun on their right". For the historian, "this fact does not seem credible, but maybe it is for others. Thus, Libya was known". The change of east side, which Herodotus questions for ignoring the geography of the African coast, is the greatest evidence of the success of the expedition, although it is not the only one.

In fact, whether or not he was successful in his exploratory ambitions, Necho II strengthened the maritime tradition started, centuries earlier, by the pharaoh Sesostris. The grandson of Necho II, Apries, went even further, crowning this tradition. During his reign, from 589 to 570 BC, the Egyptian war fleet commanded the Mediterranean. Apries' naval domain extended to the point where his navy took the city of Tyre, defeating the skilled Phoenician sailors at sea. After Apries, Egypt fell silent. More than fifty years after his death in 525 BC, the country was conquered by the Persians

Persian rule had positive periods, such as that of Darius I (521 – 486 BC), who faced resistance from the Egyptian princes of the Delta region. In the end, the Egyptians were finally defeated, at the time of Amyrtaeus, the only king of the 28th dynasty who revolted against Persian power.

For a brief period, Nectanebo I (380 BC), the first king of the thirtieth dynasty, managed to reconquer the country's independence. The pharaohs of this dynasty strove to restore Egypt to its former glory, especially in cultural, religious and institutional terms. However, the Persians returned to dominate the country in 343 BC and kept in the

Herodotus, the "Father of History", narrated the expedition ordered by the pharaoh Necho II (statue of Herodotus in Vienna, Austria).

leadership of Egypt until the conquest of Alexander, in 332 BC. From then on, Egyptian culture is absorbed and mixed with Hellenic ways and manners.

Alexander, conqueror of Egypt, in a Roman mosaic depicting the Battle of Gaugamela, against the Persians.

Egyptian Periods and Dynasties

Dynasties	Period
I-II	Protodynastic Period (c. 3200 – 2665 BC)
III-VIII	Old Kingdom (2664 – 2155 BC)
IX-XI	First Intermediate Period (2154 – 2052 BC)
XII	Middle Kingdom (2052 – 1786 BC)
XIII-XVII	Second Intermediate Period (1785 – 1554 BC)
XVIII-XX	New Kingdom (1554 – 1075 BC)

Source: The Legacy of Egypt, R.A. Parker, J.R. Harris editor, Oxford, 1971)

The Egyptian Religion

The meaning of the word "religion", from the Latin religare, is to reconnect the divine essence of man to his ego, that is, to enable the meeting between the ego and the divine spark that exists in all of us – which the Inuit Eskimos call "Great Man", evangelicals call "Christ" and Hindus call "Atman". This concept is the core of all religions and is modernly known as the "Perennial Philosophy".

The term "Perennial Philosophy" was first used by a German Christian writer of the 16th century and subsequently explored by the philosopher Leibniz (1646 – 1716) and the English novelist and playwright Aldous Huxley (1894 – 1963). In Huxley's book, entitled The Perennial Philosophy, the author says that the rudiments of perennial philosophy are "in the traditional knowledge of primitive people in all regions of the world, and, in its highest and most developed forms, in each one of the highest religions". Hence the name "perennial philosophy": it is

Philosopher Gottfried Leibniz explored and broadened the reach of the term "Perennial Philosophy".

a perception common to all humanity that arises in different times and places, but always with the same essence. "A version of this highest common denominator of all preceding and subsequent theologies," Huxley continues, "was first put in writing more than twenty-five centuries ago, and since that time the inexhaustible theme has been treated countless times, from the point of view of each religious tradition and in all main languages of Asia and Europe".

In terms of doctrine, the Perennial Philosophy is the "metaphysics that recognizes the substantial divine Reality in the world of things, lives and minds; it is the psychology that finds in the soul something similar to the divine Reality, or identical to it; it is the ethics that places man's final term in the knowledge of the immanent and transcendent foundation of all being".

In addition to this core, formal religion has other characteristics. Huston Smith, author of the bestseller The World's Religions: Our Great Wisdom Traditions, points out the six aspects that characterize all religions. "These aspects appear with such regularity that they suggest their seeds are part of the human constitution," Smith said. They are:

• **Authority**: all religions have this aspect, represented by institutions, administrative bodies, people imbued with high positions in a given hierarchy.

• **Ritual:** it is the cradle of the religion, the celebration of the integration between the human and the divine. The mythologist Joseph Campbell (1904 – 1987) maintained that "the ritual is the enactment of the myth". The myths, which play a fundamental role in religions, bring in their content access keys to understanding the mystical universe.

• **Speculation:** religions seek to answer questions such as "where do we come from", "who are we", "what are we doing here", "where do we go after death".

• **Tradition:** it is also the role of religions to transmit wisdom from generation to generation. This aspect led some authors to refer to them as "wisdom traditions".

• **Grace:** it is the belief that reality is on our side. The Universe is friendly and corroborates our evolution.

• **Mystery:** religions celebrate and carry with them the mystery that is beyond our reach. Our mind is finite. It cannot, therefore, measure the infinity to which it is connected. The religions are a bridge to this mystery.

As one of the first organized religions of humanity, Egyptian religion included all of these aspects. Its precepts and doctrines are equally rooted in the Perennial Philosophy. Its concepts and beliefs greatly influenced future doctrines, including the Christian one, which adopted the idea of existence after death and the need to preserve the body of the dead (although, among Christians, the reason for preservation is the resurrection of the body at the Last Judgment). In addition to the theological aspect itself, its belief in life after death and its conception of the origin of the Universe, the Egyptian religion can be seen as a state religion, strongly conditioned by the characteristics of each dynasty. There was also a popular religion, which revolved around superstitions and magical practices.

The Egyptians conceived a cosmic order that extended to human life and social order. Who kept this cosmic order was the pharaoh. His acts influenced the Maat, that is, universal harmony. However, over time, belief in the sacred nature of the pharaoh was gradually losing credibility and people no longer trusted in a promising immortality.

Life Beyond the Grave

Egyptian culture was based on the notion of a world created with an unchanging form. Even the observed changes were interpreted as cyclical and belonging to a fixed model, which did not change. This thought originated the concept that death was seen as part of a cyclical process. For common people, death was understood as a passage from this world to the next. For the pharaoh, however, it was believed that the god Horus transferred from the dead king to his successor. In this way, despite physical death, the Egyptians believed in immortality.

The conviction of eternal life following death and its concern with this survival of the spirit became one of the basic concepts of Egyptian religion and culture. At the beginning of Egyptian civilization, immortality was considered a prerogative of the pharaoh and granted to others who would continue to serve the king after their earthly lives. Gradually, however, immortality was assigned to the nobility and finally, to all individuals.

The Egyptians' idea about the existence after death is very complex and underwent changes over time. However, some concepts were always present. One of them is that the afterlife is dependent on the preservation of the body, literally, that is, through mummification, or through images, considered a substitute for the body. The tomb was necessary to keep the body and images of the dead. Another idea that is always present in Egyptian religion is that the three components of the soul, that is, Ka, the vital principle, Ba, the psychic factor, and Akh, its manifestation after death, had a material manifestation, although impalpable and able to pass through any obstacle.

Depiction of a priest making offerings to the Ka of a dead person.

It is hard to define the idea of Ka. Maybe what comes closest to the original concept is that of a spiritual double, a metaphysical, invisible, volatile element that allowed the existence of humans and secured eternal life after death. It was the essence, the vital substance, that distinguishes the living being from the dead.

Another spiritual principle of the ancient Egyptians was the Ba, a metaphysical, immaterial and invisible element that made the individual unique. After death, Ba unites with Ka, by force of Nehebkau – the energy that, after death, impels Ba and Ka to unite.

Ideas about the kind of life people led in the other world varied according to a person's social situation, but changed as Egyptian civilization developed over time. In the Old Kingdom, the existence after death was understood as the reintegration of the dead ones into the cosmic process. Thus, the dead pharaoh would become incorporated into the Sun, Aten-Re, or, in common people, the *Ba* of the deceased

Ba birds in the temple of goddess Hathor in Dendera, Egypt.

person would be transformed into Akh, which, in turn, would be transformed into a star in the sky – especially in the circumpolar region of the firmament.

From the first intermediate period, the quality of existence after death started being associated with the type of life that the individual led. It was a period of spiritual revolution. From then on, immortality, which was previously a privilege of the god-king, started being attributed to all human beings. Everyone started identifying with Osiris and having a personal life in the fields of Aaru, or "fields of reeds", the place where they would spend eternity, among the stars, or in the Western Lands. Here the dead had a happy existence. They could cultivate the fields they chose, helped by the good spirits, the ushbetti, in a mild climate, where they satisfied themselves by loving, having children and resting – an idyllic, simple, happy earthly life without the adversities we fear so much. There was, however, the danger that the dead would be overpowered before the soul reached Aaru, which required special amulets to be placed on the corpse and the tomb to defend it and to be welcomed by Osiris.

To the extent that Egyptian civilization fell into decay, also the vision of the land of the dead grew darker. At that time, the fields of Aaru became the harsh, sad and dark west. Instead of the optimistic images that adorned the tombs of ancient times, in the final centuries of Egyptian civilization, tomb art reinforced the expectation of the dangers that surrounded the dead and the negative aspects of death. As a result, magical resources and appeal to the gods' mercy increase.

Despite the concern with the existence after death, the Egyptians sought happiness. in his A Critical Study of History, writes that "although immersed in the conception of an immutable reality, the Egyptians were a pragmatic people, able to adjust to changing circumstances and were strongly oriented towards personal happiness and the enjoyment of life". According to the historian, this was possible because the Egyptians combined their pragmatic characteristic regarding external circumstances (drought, plagues, diseases, etc.) with their vision of an immutable Cosmos due to their way of thinking, based on two concepts: consubstantiality and the multiple identity.

Reconstitution by computer graphics of a pharaoh's burial chamber.

According to the notion of consubstantiality, a thing can manifest itself in another form, however maintaining the original substance. Hence the idea of multiple identity, which admits that a thing can have several forms, without, however, losing its identity. Thus, the gods could be or manifest themselves as people or animals.

Mummies

Life in the other world depended on the body of the dead being preserved. Normally, this was done through mummification, but also through magical images that depicted the deceased person. The rite of opening the mouth was important. Through this ritual, carried out by a priest, the senses paralyzed by death were returned to the mummy.

Preservation of the body also required that the corpse be placed in a proper tomb, to be visited by its Ka and Ba. Offerings of food and objects used in earthly life, or images of these objects, were deposited in the tombs. Some mastabas of the second dynasty even included toilets. The tomb was, thus, a necessary basis for the existence after death.

Depiction of the mummification process in ancient Egypt, including the god Anubis.

Egyptian mummy in open sarcophagus.

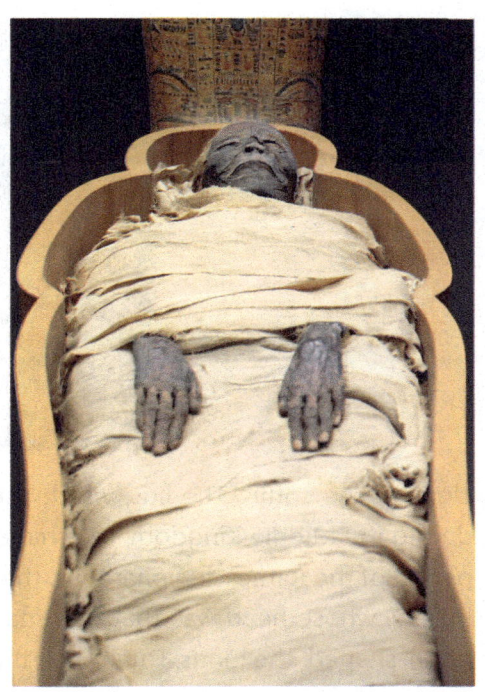

The *Ka*, the spiritual double, could survive indefinitely if the body was preserved. For this reason, the corpse should be embalmed by a specialist. Mummification was carried out in workshops attached to the necropolis, which also disposed of most of the funerary utensils. The methods varied with the time and the degree of wealth of the deceased's family.

Although there is no detailed description of this process, the stages of embalming can be reconstituted by examining the mummies. The whole process took about seventy days and the most important part of it was dehydrating the body, which they did by immersing the corpse in a natron solution, a natural dehydrating agent composed of hydrated sodium carbonate. The viscera were removed through a small incision in the side of the abdomen, and the brain was removed through the nose with a special instrument. The internal organs were placed in appropriate containers, called canopic jars, usually made of alabaster, but also of other materials such as limestone, ceramics or earthenware. The canopic jars were placed in the burial chamber of the pyramid or tomb,

Canopic jars.

close to the coffin. The lids, which used to be simple, started having, during the Middle Kingdom, the shape of a human head and, from the period of the Ramesside pharaohs, the heads of the four sons of Horus. Imsety, whose head was that of a man, contained the liver; Hapy, baboon-shaped, the lungs; Duamutef, the jackal, the stomach; and Qebehsenuef, the falcon, the intestines. The heart remained in the body and the brain was destroyed, since the ancient Egyptians did not attribute a specific function to this organ.

Mummy of a pharaoh. Over the chest, a protection in the shape of a shield invokes Horus.

Analysis of embalmed mummies at the end of New Kingdom and during the Third Intermediate Period reveals the following steps:

1. Extraction of the brain;
2. Removal of the viscera through an incision in the left side;
3. Sterilization of body cavities and viscera;
4. Treatment of viscera: removal of its contents, dehydration with natron, drying, anointing and application of melted resin;
5. Filling of the body with natron and scented resins;
6. Covering the body with natron for about forty days;
7. Removal of filling materials;
8. Subcutaneous filling of the members with sand, clay, etc.
9. Filling the body cavities with cloths soaked in resin and bags of aromatic substances, such as myrrh, cinnamon and others;
10. Anointing the body with ointments;
11. Treatment of the body surface with melted resin;
12. Bandaging, which includes placing amulets, jewelry and other ornaments and religious objects.

The tomb should be made of stone, so as to constitute an impenetrable barrier to protect the body. Normally, a secret passage led to a chamber, provided with food, weapons, equipment, with figures of servants, carved or painted, which, by means of magical formulas uttered by the priests, would accompany and serve forever the body and the *Ka*.

The interior of the body was purified, washed with wine and treated with perfumes and aromatic spices. Then, the body was sunk in antiseptic substances, rubbed with adhesive resin and carefully bandaged. When this process was complete, the mummy was placed in a skiff on whose lid its image had been painted.

The sarcophagus lids reproduced the person's face in life. In this way, its Ka could recognize the body to which it was connected.

The Religion of the Mysteries

Another peculiarity of the Egyptian religion is the so-called "Religion of the Mysteries", which was one of the radiating centers in Antiquity. These initiatory practices ended up giving rise, over time, to secret societies that continued to exist throughout history, such as Freemasonry.

The Mysteries consisted of a group of beliefs and practices that existed in many countries under different forms. In Egypt they were the

Temple of Isis on Lake Nasser, where the mysteries of this goddess were celebrated.

Mysteries of Isis and Osiris; in Greece, the Mysteries of Dionysus and Eleusis; in Rome, the Mysteries of Bacchus and Ceres. Many of the great minds of that time, such as the philosopher Pythagoras, were initiated in one or more of these schools of wisdom.

Nothing pure remains of this knowledge. The initiations, made through oral tradition, were lost or corrupted over the centuries. Fermented by the secret that embraced the initiations, strange stories and bizarre rumors were related to them.

The testimony of classical authors shows, however, a different face of the Mysteries. The tragic poet Sophocles wrote that "three times happy are the mortals who descend into the realms of Hades after having contemplated the Mysteries". Plato also testified about the sanctity of the initiations. In Phaedo (or On the Soul), where the philosopher reflects about life after death, Plato stated: "I admit that the men who established the Mysteries possessed enlightenment and that, in reality, they had a veiled intention when they said, a long time ago, that whoever goes to the other world without being initiated and sanctified will lie in the mud, but whoever arrives there initiated and purified, will live with the gods".

The tragic poet Sophocles, for whom knowledge of the mysteries was essential for the existence after death.

Cosmogonies

The Egyptian Myths

The religions approach the mystery – incomprehensible to our finite mind – making use of the language of symbols. These inspire and teach; they are the raw material of art, constituting a timeless "grammar" that allows access to spiritual truths.

In *The Cambridge Companion to Jung* (Cambridge University Press), British psychologists Polly Young-Eisendrath and Terence Dawson define symbol as follows: "the best possible expression for something that is inferred, but not directly known, or that cannot be properly defined by means of words".

A symbol should not be confused with a sign. The difference between a symbol and a sign is curious and has to do not with the depiction itself, but with the receiver of the information. For example, for a

Egyptian icons: the myths make use of the language of symbols.

Christian passing in front of a church, the cross on top of its campanile is a symbol that expresses the ineffable mystery of Christ's sacrifice. However, if the person passing in front of the church is a Buddhist or a Muslim, the cross will only be a sign, indicating that there is a meeting place for people of the Christian faith.

Every religion incorporates in its precepts a collection of myths, which are intended for specific purposes. This is so clear that it led the president of the Joseph Campbell Foundation, Robert Walter, to state, jokingly, that "myth is the religion of the other". Maybe it sounds weird to us Westerners to hear about "Christian mythology", but the fact is that all wisdom traditions make use of myths.

Joseph Campbell, who, along with Mircea Eliade, was probably the greatest mythologist of the 20th century, noted that the myths are metaphors for life and the universe that basically fulfill four functions. The first of them is the mystical function, which encompasses the perception and evocation of the mystery that surrounds us. "The myth opens the world to the dimension of mystery," Campbell stated.

The second function of the myth deals with the cosmological dimension, a role that today is restricted to science. The myths, like science, also seek to explain the origin and nature of things.

The third function is the sociological one. The myth supports and validates a certain social order. And this is where the myths vary tremendously from place to place. "You have a whole mythology related to polygamy and a whole mythology related to monogamy," Campbell said. "Anyone could be right; it just depends on where you are"!

It is this sociological function of the myth that establishes ethical laws – like those established by the Hebrew prophets of the Old Testament –, laws that determine how to behave, what to wear, eat and the relationship between the sexes.

The fourth function of the myth is the pedagogical one. The myths contain important lessons, which show how to live life in a wise and fruitful way.

The myths are made up of cosmogonies – histories about the origin of the Universe – and of the gods who ordered chaos and ordered the Cosmos. The Egyptians had three cosmogonies, from which their myths and gods derived, ordering the life and relationships of their society.

Heliopolis

The first one – and most fundamental – was that of Heliopolis. In the beginning there was Nun, a liquid, uncontrolled element that represented chaos. It was an uncreated substance that had all the possi-

Scarab Beetle: Egyptian sacred bug, symbol of the sun.

Goddess Nut, the sky, embraces Geb, the god of the Earth, forming the celestial vault.

bilities of life. The souls that did not receive the benefit of funeral rites and the stillborn inhabited Nun. From this chaos emerged Atum, the Sun, created by himself. He appeared on a mound of earth that had emerged out of the waters. Atum masturbated and from his semen two gods were created, Shu the Dry and Tefnut the Moist. These gods united and gave rise to the goddess Nut, the Sky, and the god Geb, the Earth. Nut and Geb had four children: Isis, Osiris, Set and Nephthys.

Hermopolis

The cosmogony of Hermopolis describes the emergence of the Ogdoad, the set of eight supreme gods, made up of divine couples: Nun and Naunet, the Primordial Ocean; Heh and Hauhet, the Infinite Space; Kek and Kauket, the Darkness; and the fourth couple was Amun, the hidden god, and Amunet, the Air. The name of the goddesses is the feminine of the name of the gods. In fact, these gods represented the male and female aspects that formed the four primordial elements, from which everything originated - the Primitive Ocean, the Infinite Space, the Darkness and the Air.

Memphis

According to the cosmogony of Memphis , Ptah was the god of creation who shaped human beings with clay. Ptah was succeeded by Ra, dispelling darkness and creating life.

These cosmogonies originated three main lines of cult, with specific clergy, in different cities. In Thebes, Amun, the Hidden One, had his main center of the cult. The seat of Ra, the Sun, was Heliopolis, and Ptah, the Creator, was worshiped in Memphis. The Egyptian dynasties ended up influencing the aspect of these deities. Under the influence of the Theban dynasty, Amun was associated with Ra, becoming Amun-Ra, recognized as the supreme god. Over time, Theban theology started admitting only three gods, the trinity Amun, Ra and Ptah. Amun was his name, to the extent that he hid himself. Ra was his face and Ptah, his body. Some specialists have argued the fact that the Theban trinity anticipated the Christian one

The Myth of Osiris

One of the most important elements of Egyptian mythology is the history of the death and rebirth of Osiris, which revolve around the other elements of Egyptian religion.

The god Ptah with the pharaoh Seti, in the temple of Osiris, in Abydos.

Relief in the temple of Horus showing the pharaoh (incarnation of that god) slaughtering Set.

In ancient times, long before the construction of the great pyramids, the god Osiris reigned over Egypt as the first pharaoh. It was a time of happiness and abundance. He and his queen, the goddess Isis, taught men agriculture and all other arts. Their happy subjects were grateful to them and venerated them.

But Osiris' brother, Set, the god of mischief, started being jealous of the pharaoh's success. Scheming to make his brother disappear and take his place as emperor of Egypt, Set invited Osiris to a feast. But it was a trap.

Set caught his brother, tied him up and placed him inside a wooden chest. Then, he threw the chest into the River Nile, thinking that the crocodiles would put an end to the unwanted Osiris.

The people became very sad with the disappearance of the pharaoh. And according to the law, the throne of Egypt passed to Set.

The faithful Isis, however, did not lose hope of finding her husband and went looking for him all over the world.

After much traveling and looking, Isis finally managed to find the chest where Osiris was trapped. The king of Byblos – an important Phoenician city of Gebal – found it by chance and kept it in his palace. He did not know what it contained, as he had failed to open it. Isis told the king of Byblos about the contents of the ark. With her power, the goddess freed Osiris.

But Set stepped in again. This time, the envious god of mischief was even more cruel. To get rid of his brother for good, he killed Osiris and cut his body into fourteen pieces, which he threw into the River Nile.

Not even that made Isis give up. With the help of Anubis, the god with a jackal head, protector of the dead, Isis recovered all the pieces of Osiris' body. So, she and Anubis resurrected Osiris. For this, they made the first mummy, that of Osiris, and carried out powerful rituals that revived him.

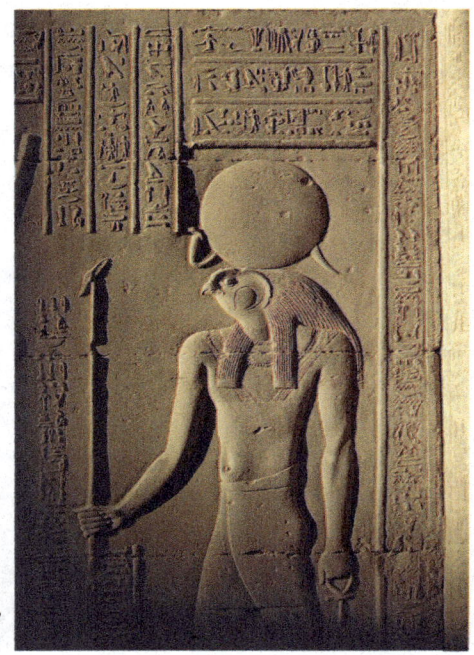

Horus, in relief in the temple of Kom Ombo.

He tried and failed to recover Egypt's throne before Set devastated the country even more. Osiris, however, only managed this through his son Horus.

Ever since he was a child, Horus wanted to avenge his father. When he became an adult, he took the case to the court of the gods, who decided in his favor. But not even then Set gave in. Horus was forced to fight his uncle. In the end, he managed to reconquer the kingdom to which he was entitled.

As soon as the new pharaoh took the throne, the country was covered in green again, and its people were happy again.

Osiris then decided to leave for the Kingdom of the Dead, where he continued to reign.

From then on, the Egyptians started venerating each of their pharaohs as Horus, the falcon god, and, after being dead and mummified, as Osiris, the Lord of the Dead.

Tuat
Tuat, or Duat, was a vast region under the earth, connected with Nun, the waters of the primordial abyss. It was the realm

Tomb of a pharaoh.

Gods and entities of ancient Egypt.

of Osiris, the underworld inhabited by the souls of the dead. At night, the god Ra – the Sun – travels from west to east through the Tuat, where he faces fearsome demons and his greatest enemy, the serpent Apep, which he always kills, but which is reborn to fight the god again at night.

The tombs are portals that communicate the world of the living to Tuat. The texts about Tuat that came to us, belonging to different periods, give a different perspective on this mythical world. As with everything related to the long history of Egyptian civilization, the concept of the Tuat also changed over time.

The geography of this region is similar to the world the Egyptians knew. There are rivers, islands, fields, lakes, mountains and caves; there are also fantastic locations in the realm of Osiris, such as lakes of fire, iron walls and gemstone trees.

Egyptian priests wrote a travel itinerary, the Book of the Dead, to guide souls through the Tuat and warn them of the dangers that awaited them in this place. The dead had to pass through a series of gates guarded by dangerous spirits – anthropo-zoomorphic beings, with the bodies of men and women and the heads of animals, who threatened the traveling spirits. In this way, the text describes a series of rites of passage that the dead would have to go through in order to conquer the existence after death.

The souls that managed to face the dangers of the path without being destroyed would reach a hall, where they would be judged. To this end, their hearts were weighed by Anubis, before Osiris. The counterweight used by Anubis was a feather, given by Maat, the goddess of truth and justice. The heart of someone who did not follow Maat in life was heavier than the feather and the spirits in this condition were devoured by Ammit, the Devourer of Souls. Those souls who passed the test would be allowed to continue their trip to Aaru, or "Field of Reeds" – the paradise of the Egyptians.

The Egyptian Gods

The Egyptian Deities

The Egyptian gods were anthropo-zoomorphic, that is, they had the shape of animals and humans – usually, but not always, men or women with animal heads. As was common within Antiquity, the same gods assumed different aspects in the several cities where they were worshiped. They were local – or, as in the case of Greece, national – gods, patrons of the cities that celebrated them. Thus, when the kingdoms

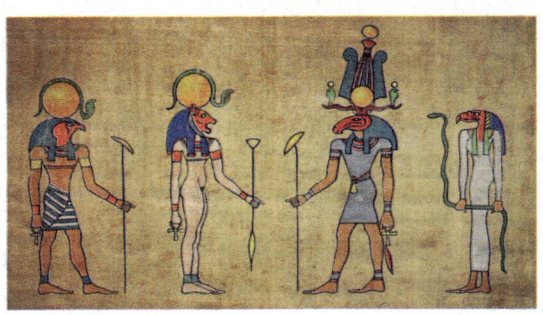

The Egyptian gods were anthropo-zoomorphic, that is, they had human and animal characteristics.

The gods Anubis, Set, Horus and Hathor

along the Nile were unified, new gods ended up merging with older ones. This also caused the consorts of certain gods varied from region to region and from era to era, giving rise to legends about the adulteries of the gods.

As in the Hindu religion, the Egyptians had countless gods and goddesses, worshiped in different places. Some of them took on greater importance; others were celebrated only in some places. Over thousands of years, the Egyptian pantheon was being changed, becoming extremely complex.

For the Egyptians, in the beginning there was a supreme, eternal, immortal, omniscient, omnipresent and omnipotent being. This primordial principle, called "neter", unfolded in several aspects, the neteru. The word is nothing more than the plural of "neter". The neteru have, each one, attributes that govern and maintain the cosmic order. These neteru are the Egyptian gods, created from such original cosmogonic principle, the neter. There are the primordial neteru (Nun, Atum, Amun, Aten, Ra, Ptah, Hu). Then there are the generator neteru (Shu, Tefnut, Geb, Nut). There were also the first generation neteru (Osiris, Isis, Set and Nephthys), the second generation neteru (Horus, Hathor, Thoth, Maat, Anubis, Anuket, Bastet, Sokar, Sekhmet) and other minor neteru (Mafdet, Nekhbet, Serket, Sobek, Meretseger, Iah, Montu, Wadjet, Bes, Hapi). In addition to them, the ancient Egyptian religion also worshiped animal gods (Apis, Ammit, Mnevis, Bennu) and deified humans (Amenhotep, Imhotep).

The Egyptian gods belonged to divine families, forming what the Greeks called Enneads (or pesedjet, in Egyptian), that is, a grouping of nine deities, usually connected to each other by family ties. The most important Ennead was that of Heliopolis.

According to the cosmogony of that city, in the beginning there were only the waters of the primordial abyss, and Nun, from which a hill emerged, on which stood a god who had generated himself, Atum. The god masturbated and, from his semen, other deities were born, Shu (the air) and Tefnut (the moisture). The couple of brothers, in turn, generated Geb (the earth) and Nut (the sky), who also united and created Osiris, Isis, Set, Horus and Nephthys, thus forming the first ennead. Other Enneads, such as that of Abydos and Thebes, were made up of not of nine gods, but of seven and fifteen, respectively. There was also

Relief with an image of Isis and Osiris in the Temple of Osiris, in Abydos.

the "Little Ennead of Heliopolis" made up of Thoth, Anubis, Maat and Khnum.

The Gods and Their Attributes
Amenhotep (son of Hapu)

Amenhotep was a deified human. Like the Catholic saints who, because they led an exemplary life, reached divine status, the ancient Egyptians also attributed a sacred character to those who conquered great achievements. It was believed that they were like the divine expression in a given man. Amenhotep, known as "son of Hapu" (1440 BC - 1360 BC) was a vizier of the pharaoh Amenhotep III during the 18th dynasty of Egypt. From humble origin, Amenhotep started his career as a scribe. A competent architect, he supervised, among other works, the Colossi of Memnon, as the Greeks called the stone statues of the pharaoh Amenhotep III. The pharaoh showed his gratitude to the vizier by dedicating

The pharaoh Amenhotep III, lord of the deified architect Amenhotep, making a libation on a relief of the Temple of Amun, in Karnak, Luxor, Egypt.

Sphinxes with the head of ram in the Temple of Amun, in Karnak.

a statue to him in his temple of Karnak, which represented a great honor, especially because Amenhotep was a plebeian. He died at the age of eighty and was buried in a tomb carved into the rock, on the banks of the Nile in Thebes. By being deified, he was considered a deity related to healing, and was associated with Osiris and Amun-Ra. He was depicted as a man holding a papyrus scroll.

Ammit

The fearsome Ammit is the personification of divine retribution for all evils done in life. It was the dog of the court of Osiris, where the final judgment was held, when the heart of the dead was placed on the scales of Osiris and the weight revealed its acts in life. If the soul was bad, it was devoured by Ammit, ceasing to exist forever. Papyri have been found with prayers to ward off Ammit during sleep.

Amun

Amun, (also Amon, Ammon, Amen or in Egyptian Yamānu, "The Hidden One"), was one of the main Egyptian deities, the king of the gods and the creative force of life. God originating from Karnak, he had Mut as a consort, in whom he generated Khonsu. His main cult center was Thebes.

Amun, although identified with the sun, was depicted in several different forms: an animal, a man's body and an animal's head, or a man wearing a cap adorned with two large feathers.

Amun offering the ankh, symbol of life, to the pharaoh Thutmose IV.

Sometimes he was depicted as a goose or a ram, animals associated with him. His priests had their heads shaved and wore white tunics with leopard skin capes. The priests of Amun came to accumulate so much power that the pharaoh Amenhotep IV, later Akhenaten, replaced his cult with that of Aten. However, he was not successful.

Anput

Anput was the wife of the god Anubis and mother of the goddess Kebechet.

Anubis

Anubis was the Greek name for the Egyptian god Inpu, with a jackal head, associated with mummification and the existence after death. He was the son of Nephthys, wife of Set, who, during a fight with her husband, pretended to be Isis and had relations with Osiris, conceiving the jackal god.

Anubis was one of the oldest deities in Egyptian mythology and his role changed in different periods of that civilization's history. In the Old Kingdom, Anubis was the most important god of the dead. However, in the Middle Kingdom, he gave way to Osiris. His funeral function continued, however. It was Anubis who weighed the hearts of the dead against the Feather of Truth on the scales of Osiris. And if the heart were lighter than the feather, it was also he who guided the souls of the dead to the Beyond. As it was Anubis who embalmed the body of Osiris, thus creating the first

The god Anubis.

mummy, and inventing the mummification process, he was also the god of embalming. Identified with the jackal, probably because it is an animal that attends cemeteries, the priests of Anubis wore jackal masks during the rituals they carried out.

In his depictions, Anubis was painted black, because the tone of the embalmed bodies was dark. The wife of Anubis, his female aspect, was Anput and his daughter was Kebechet.

Amunet

Identified by the Greeks as the goddess Athena, Amunet was the female aspect of Amun. Like her consort, her name means "The Hidden One". Both represented the intangible, what is hidden, and the power that is not extinguished. In some depictions, Amunet appears as a woman with a frog's head; in others like a cow. Amunet played an important role in the pharaoh's crowning ceremonies.

Hieroglyphs in an Egyptian tomb.

Anuket

Anuket, or Anukis, was a deity initially linked to water; later she became a goddess associated with sexuality. Like water, which surrounds everything, her name means, precisely, "to embrace". Khnum's wife, her cult was centered on the island of Sehel. She was depicted as a woman wearing a headdress adorned with feathers or plants, or else as a gazelle – the animal associated with her. The Ptolemaic related her to Hestia, the Greek goddess of the home.

Apep

Apep, or Apophis, as the Greeks called it, is the gigantic serpent enemy of Ra, who fought him every night, trying to destroy the god's boat. Although Ra always killed it, Apep invariably resurrected. Served by hordes of demons in the form of fiery serpents, Apep personifies the chaos of the underworld and the resulting annihilation of this chaos. Therefore, Apep is a sworn enemy of the gods, who are its counterpart, since they order the Cosmos.

The Egyptians believed that, when there was an eclipse, it was the gigantic body of Apep that covered the light, when trying to destroy the boat of Ra (as they called the Sun) and devour him.

Image of Apep, god of the underworld and chaos.

Pharaoh with the head of a bull (Apis), in the temple of Horus in Edfu, Egypt.

A late myth told that, in the end, Ra trapped Apep in the depths of the Tuat with Bastet, the cat goddess, or, in some versions, with Sekhmet, the lioness goddess, in a brutal and eternal fight. Other variations of this myth state that the god trapped the enemy in a sea of scarab beetles that were in Tuat.

Apis

Apis – Hapi-ankh, for the Egyptians –, the personification of the Earth, was the incarnation of Osiris in a white bull, the bull of Memphis, symbolically depicted as a white bull or, then, black with a white triangle on the forehead.

Aten

Aten was one of the most important Egyptian gods. He was the solar disk, worshiped by the pharaoh Akhenaten, who imposed his cult to the detriment of other gods, especially Amun.

The solar disk, symbol of Aten.

Atum, an Egyptian god worshiped in Heliopolis.

Atum

Atum, worshiped in Heliopolis, is the transformation of Nun – the subjective being – into the objective being. He was a primordial god and creator: it was he who caused the explosion that generated the other beings of the Universe. Atum created the evening sun, and when he "became himself", he changed into Ra and became Atum-Ra. Thisgod, in turn, generated by himself the first neteru, the twins Shu (god of air) and Tefnut (goddess of moisture), and created the morning sun. Then he created the sky and the earth and separated them. The brothers, in turn, united and had a couple of children, Geb (god of the earth) and Nut (goddess of the skies). Ra's grandchildren also united - which displeased their grandfather. Thus, Ra ordered Shu to separate his children. Shu pushed Nut up and pressed Geb down. While Nut became the sky that covers the world, Geb became the land we live on. Shu, the air we breathe, remained among his children.

Bastet

Bastet, the feline goddess, also called Bast, Ubaste, Ba-en-A-set or Ailuros, which in Greek means "cat", was a solar deity, goddess of fertility and protector of women. In the Ptolemaic period, the Greek invaders associated Bastet with Artemis, goddess of the moon and the forests. Because of this, Bastet started being a lunar goddess. The goddess was seen as a woman with a head of cat, carrying a sistrum (sacred musical instrument). In some depictions, she had a basket, where she placed her young, or she could be painted or sculpted as a simple cat.

The goddess Bastet, one of the daughters of Ra.

Sometimes, she assumed the attributes of Sekhmet, acquiring the fierce aspect of a lioness. Like the Hindu goddess Kali – the feminine principle that generates as much as it destroyed – this aspect of the goddess was indeed angry. One time, Ra ordered Sekhmet to punish men due to their disobedience. The goddess punished humanity with such brutality that Ra had to get her drunk, making her sleep, so that she would not end up exterminating the entire human race. Thus, sleeping Sekhmet was the cat, meek and domestic, Bastet – her other side.

Her cult center was the city of Bubastis, in the Nile Delta. Her temples were true catteries, where cats, considered the incarnation of the goddess, were treated with great attention and care. When the animals died, they were mummified and buried in their own necropolis. Several of these animal cemeteries were discovered by archaeologists.

Bat

Bat, the cow, is one of the oldest deities of the Egyptian pantheon, worshiped since the end of the Paleolithic, when the domestication of animals started, in this case, oxen and cows. But Bat also had an anthropo-zoomorphic aspect. Sometimes she was portrayed with a human face, cow ears and horns. At the time of the Middle Kingdom, her identity and her attributes were embodied by the goddess Hathor.

Anubis holding the crux ansata (ankh) related to the sistrum, sacred instrument of Bat.

Bat became strongly associated with the sistrum, an Egyptian musical instrument often used in cults and religious celebrations. The sistrum was similar in shape to the ankh – the crux ansata, a hieroglyph that represents the word "life", a symbol of eternal life. The center of her cult was known as the "Mansion of Sistrum".

Bennu

Bennu was an animal deity, the heron. His name derived from the Egyptian verb "to shine", and the heron symbolized the Ba of the god Ra – the sun, like Atum –, when he appeared, at the moment of the creation of the world. Inversely, the bird was also seen as the Ba of Osiris, when the god was murdered by Set. The Greek invaders associated Bennu with the phoenix. According to them, Bennu appeared only every five hundred years and made a fire in which he perished and, from the ashes, arose again as a new bird.

The bird Bennu, like the phoenix, reborn from its own ashes.

Bes, the deity of joy, in the Temple of Hathor

Bes

Bes, deity of pleasure and joy, was a fat, monstrous dwarf. He was the court jester of the gods. He was the only member of the Egyptian pantheon depicted from the front, rather than in profile, as is a rule in the art of this civilization. He was associated with childbirth and children. When women were giving birth, it was believed that Bes danced, shaking his rattle and screaming to scare away demons that could harm the child. After the birth, Bes stayed next to the crib entertaining the baby. When the child laughed for no apparent reason, it was said that Bes was present, making faces to cheer the baby up.

Geb

Geb, or Seb, the god of the earth, son of Shu and Tefnut, husband of Nut and father of Osiris, Isis, Set and Nephthys, is one of the primordial deities of ancient Egypt. He was always lying under the curve of his wife's body, Nut, in the sky. One of his attributes was to imprison evil spirits so that they could not go to heaven. For this reason, he was equally a god of death. As god of the earth, the physical support of the world, he secures material wealth and assures men a burial in the ground after death. Their colors were green – the color of life – and black – the fertile mud of the Nile. He was responsible for fertility and good harvests. Associated with the goose, he was always depicted with one of these birds over his head.

Relief with the image of the god Hapi wearing a lotus crown, in the temple of the pharaoh Seti I.

Hapi

Hapi, or Hapy, a deity related to the River Nile and protector of the north direction, was one of the four sons of Horus, who protected the throne of Osiris in the afterworld. Hapi was depicted as a mummified human with a head of a baboon. He had one of the canopic jars, where the mummy's organs were deposited. Hapi's jar kept the lung.

Hathor

Hathor, or "house of Horus", is one of the most prominent goddesses in the Egyptian pantheon. She personified the principles of love, beauty, music, dance, motherhood and joy. Her maternal aspect gave her the attribute of being protector of women during childbirth and also related her to female fertility. The "Lady of the West", as she was invoked on the tombs, was one of the most popular deities of ancient Egypt, worshiped by both the nobility and the common people. It was Hathor who welcomed the dead into the afterlife.

The cult of Hathor dates back to prehistoric times. From the beginning, she was depicted as a divine cow, with a solar disk between her horns. The Greeks identified her with Aphrodite and, in Heliopolis, she manifested herself as Nebethetepet, the "lady of the offering".

Hathor is the mother and sometimes daughter and wife of Ra. In one myth, she appears as the eye of Ra. As Ra's mother, she gave birth to him every morning, and as his wife, she conceived him through the union with the god every day.

The chapel of Hathor, in the temple of the female pharaoh Hatshepsut.

Hathor was also a celestial deity, associated with the goddess Nut, with whom she represented the Milky Way. The four legs of the celestial cow were the pillars on which the sky rested, with the stars in her belly forming the Milky Way, through which the solar boat of Ra – the Sun – sailed. One of Hathor's alternative names, Mehturt, or "great flood", made reference to this association with the Milky Way, seen by the ancient Egyptians as a channel of water that crossed the firmament, the "Nile in the Sky", through which sailed both the sun and the moon. This attribute led Mehturt to be responsible for the annual flooding of the Nile. Another consequence of her aquatic aspect was to announce births, when the amniotic sac ruptures, releasing its liquid – its "waters". As the Milky Way, she was equally the primordial serpent, Wadjet – another aspect of the mother goddess.

In the fusion that took place between divinities worshiped in prehistoric times from different regions along the Nile, Hathor also identified with another cow, ancient goddess of fertility, Bat. And, like Bat, she was also related to Ba, one of the components of the soul, and ended up being linked to existence after death. With her maternal aspect, Hathor, in her character of Lady of the Necropolis, received the souls of the dead in the Tuat – the underworld, where Osiris reigns – and gave them food and drink.

Another view of the chapel of Hathor in the temple of Hatshepsut.

The cult to Hathor was centered in Dendera, in Upper Egypt, and, due to the goddess' relationship with music, it was officiated by dancing priestesses and priests, singers and artists.

Finally, Hathor was the goddess of joy and, for this very reason, was deeply loved by Egyptians of all classes, especially by women, inspired by her attributes of mother, wife and lover. More than any other Egyptian deity, several festivals were dedicated to her honor and more girls were named after her than any other goddess. As goddess of the family, both men and women could serve her as priests.

Another change that Hathor underwent over time, due to the fusion between deities of different origins, was the incorporation of the attributes of Seshat,

Hathor as the sacred cow.

goddess of writing, wife of Thoth. When she assumed this aspect, she was depicted as a woman breastfeeding her baby. As Seshat, Hathor also started being a witness in the judgment of souls in the Tuat. As she received the dead with food and drink, she also appeared as the wife of Nehebkau, guardian of the entrance to the underworld and the element which, after death, caused the Ba to unite with the Ka..

Hesat

Hesat was the earthly manifestation of Hathor, the divine cow. Like Hathor, she was also seen as the wife of Ra, in the earthly form of that god, the bull Mnevis. She was considered the wet nurse of the gods, provider of all food. Deity of abundance, she was depicted as a white cow, with milk dripping from her udders, carrying a tray of food over her horns. In some traditions, as a provider of food and therefore a giver of life, Hesat was the mother of the deity who depicted the opposite principle, Anubis, god of death. Thus, Hesat formed a familiar triad with Mnevis and Anubis, which occupied an important place in the cults of ancient Egypt.

The divine cow Hesat, relief in the Temple of Luxor in Thebes, Egypt.

Kebechet

Kebechet (Qeb-hwt), daughter of Anubis, Egyptian god of death and the dying, was the goddess of freshness and purification through water and, for this reason, ruled the embalming liquids. It was Kebechet who gave water to the spirits of the dead while they waited for the mummification process to be completed. Kebechet was depicted as a serpent – a symbol related to the feminine principle, or as a woman with the head of a snake. Sometimes, although more rarely, she was depicted as an ostrich.

Horus

The god with the head of a falcon, Horus, son of Osiris and Isis – and also the mother's husband – was the lord of the sky, the spirit of the pharaoh incarnated. With his parents, he formed the sacred family of Egypt. Isis, the mother, provider and maintainer, Horus, the Sun, the pharaoh, the governor who regulated the earth's cycles, and Osiris, the lord of the underworld, who presided over existence after death.

In his role as avenger, it was Horus who killed Set, not only to honor the death of his father, Osiris, but to take the throne of Egypt. In the fight, he lost an eye, which was replaced by the serpent amulet, the Eye of Horus, which the pharaohs started using on their crowns. The wounded eye of Horus, the left one, is the moon with its phases; the

The god Horus, spirit of the pharaoh incarnated.

The Eye of Horus, symbol of protection and power.

healthy eye is the sun. The Eye of Horus was an important symbol, the Wedjat, which, in addition to granting power, warded off the evil eye.

In one version of the history of Horus, the falcon god was conceived by Isis, when Osiris was already dead. Isis, in the form of a bird, landed on her husband's mummy, thus being impregnated.

Heh

Heh is the divinization of the first word, the word of creation, which Atum uttered when he ejaculated, when masturbating, in the act that created the Ennead – the nine original gods of Egypt. Heh was occasionally identified with Thoth, and in Ptolemaic Egypt, merged with Shu, the air.

Iah

Iah, or Aah, was the god of the moon, represented as a man, bearing the solar disk and the crescent moon on his head. He was also associated with the ibis, the falcon, the god Thoth and the god Khonsu. Several members of the Theban royal family, who expelled the Hyksos from Egypt, had Iah in their names, such as Iah-hotep I ("Aah is satisfied"), mother of Ahmose ("Iah was born"), founder of the 18th dynasty, and his wife Ahmose-Nefertari ("born of the moon, the most beautiful of women").

Imhotep

Imhotep is a historical character who was deified. Vizier of Pharaoh

Relief depicting the sacrifice of a cow, in Saqqara.

Djoser, of the third dynasty, he was considered the first architect, engineer and physician in ancient history. Of plebeian origin, from the First Intermediate Period, Imhotep also started being revered as a poet and philosopher. The location of his tomb, constructed by himself, was carefully hidden and still remains undiscovered. It is believed to be somewhere in Saqqara.

The historical existence of Imhotep is confirmed by two inscriptions: one made on the plinth of a statue of the pharaoh Djoser; the other is a reference to him on the wall surrounding the unfinished pyramid of Sekhemkhet. The second inscription suggests that Imhotep would have lived a few more years after Djoser's death and that he would have collaborated in the construction of King Sekhemkhet's pyramid.

The Step Pyramid of the pharaoh Djoser, designed by Imhotep.

Probably, the greatest achievement of Imhotep was the creation and construction of the first pyramid in Egypt – the pyramid of Saqqara, with six huge steps and a height of about 60 meters. Imhotep created the step pyramid at the request of the pharaoh Djoser, who wanted to be buried in the grandest tomb that had ever existed in Egypt. Imhotep carried out the design, including the notion of a "stairway to heaven," depicting the pharaoh's ascension to heaven.

Isis

Isis, or, in Egyptian, Auset, was one of the main deities of ancient Egypt, whose cult spread all over the Greco-Roman world. A merciful lady, goddess of maternity and fertility, she embodied the model of the ideal mother and wife, protector of nature and magic, consolation of the underprivileged, oppressed, and slaves, fishermen, artisans, and, as a provider of graces, also catered to the rich, aristocrats and rulers.

Isis, daughter of Geb, the god of the Earth, and of Nut, was the wife and sister of Osiris, with whom she had Horus. Devoted sister and a

Queen Nefertari, wife of Ramesses II, making an offering to Isis

faithful wife, with her magical skills, Isis gathered the pieces of Osiris and brought her dead husband back to life after the god had been murdered and cut to pieces by Set.

Among her many attributes, Isis was also the goddess of simplicity, protector of the dead, children, lady of magic and nature. In later myths, the annual floods of the Nile were described as the tears that Isis had shed over her husband's death. Having absorbed the attributes of several Egyptian goddesses and, when her cult spread overseas, in other nations, she was known as "Isis of the Ten Thousand Names".

In *The Golden Ass*, a work in which the Roman writer Lucius Apuleius describes the few concepts of the religion of the mysteries that survived, Isis introduces herself to the character Lucius, listing some of her attributes:

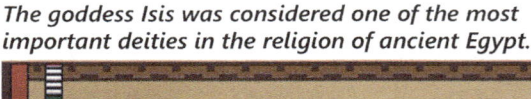

The goddess Isis was considered one of the most important deities in the religion of ancient Egypt.

"You see me here, Lucius, in answer to your prayer. I am Nature, the universal Mother, mistress of all the elements, primordial child of time, sovereign of all things spiritual, queen of the dead, queen also of the immortals, the single manifestation of all gods and goddesses that are. My nod governs the shining heights of Heaven, the wholesome sea-breezes the lamentable silences of the world below. Though I am worshipped in many aspects, known by countless names, some know me as Juno, some as Bellona of the Battles... the Egyptians who excel in ancient learning and worship me with ceremonies proper to my godhead, call me by my true name, namely, Queen Isis."

Devotion to Isis was popular throughout Egypt, although the most important sanctuaries were located in Giza and Behbeit el-Hagar in the Nile Delta, the likely origin of her cult. The importance of Isis reached its prominence in the final period of the Empire. The goddess embodied the attributes of other goddesses, who had firmly established centers of cult. During the Hellenistic and Roman periods, her cult diffused beyond the borders of Egypt, spreading both East and West. Even in Rome, where temples and obelisks were erected in her honor, the faith in this Egyptian goddess was popular. On the island of Philae, in the Upper Nile, the cult to Isis and Osiris persisted until the sixth century of our era, when Christianity was already well established. It was the only pagan temple in the Roman Empire that had been spared from the Decree of Theodosius (c. 380 AD), which determined the destruction of all pagan temples. Due to an ancient treaty signed between the priests of Philae and the emperor Diocletian (244 – 311 AD), this pagan temple was the last to be closed by the Christian emperors.

The goddess was also patroness of the Mysteries of Isis, one of the most significant branches of the religions of the mysteries, associated with death and rebirth. As the consort of Osiris, the Lord of the Dead, the goddess was associated with death. Isis was also the mother and wife of Horus, symbol of the pharaoh. For this reason, the goddess was seen as the wife, mother and protector of the king of Egypt.

A late myth tells that Isis was the foster mother of Anubis. This version attests that Set denied Nephthys a child. To seduce him, Nephthys disguised herself as Isis. The plan failed, but Osiris started wanting Nephthys and, possessing her, generated Anubis in her. Afraid of Set's reprisals, Nephthys persuaded Isis to adopt Anubis, so that the child would not be discovered and killed. As the son of the lord of the underworld and living with his father, Anubis became a deity of the underworld.

Another important aspect of Isis is that of mother – and at times, wife – of Horus. Soon after having generated him in the reconstituted body of Osiris, Isis ran away with the young Horus to escape the wrath of Set, the murderer of her husband. Once, Isis healed Horus of a scorpion sting. Under the protection of the goddess, Horus grew strong and faced Set, becoming pharaoh of Egypt.

For accomplishments such as the resurrection of Osiris and the conception of Horus, Isis is the Lady of Magic. In fact, magic – which also involves healing power – is a central element in the entire mythology of Isis, possibly more so than for any other Egyptian deity. The mastery of magic was one of the factors in the popularity of the cult of Isis. Because of her magical skills, after Egypt was occupied by the Greeks and Romans, Isis became the most important and powerful deity in the Egyp-

Relief of Isis on her throne, in the Temple of Osiris in Abydos, Egypt.

Icons of Egypt, including the pyramids of Giza, the Eye of Horus, the crux ansata and the scarab beetle, as well as the gods Anubis (left) and Hathor (right).

tian pantheon. In the ancient sky northern Africa, the star Spica ("Alpha Virginis") rose above the horizon at the time of the wheat harvest and, for this reason, was associated with fertility deities, such as Hathor. Isis would come to be seen as this star, due to the later merging of her attributes with those of Hathor. In the same way, Isis also assimilated attributes of Sopdet, personification of the star Sirius, which appears on the horizon just before the flood of the Nile. Another symbol of Isis is the rose. The fact that this goddess was so popular made the production of roses an important activity throughout Egypt.

Among the many depictions of this goddess, Isis was portrayed as a woman in a long dress and crowned with the hieroglyph that meant "throne". She was also portrayed carrying a lotus or under a sycamore tree. When she assimilated the attributes of Hathor, Isis started being portrayed crowned with the insignia of Hathor: the horns of a cow, with the sun disk between them. Sometimes, she was also depicted as a cow, or a head of a cow. She was, however, almost always depicted with her young son, Horus (the pharaoh), wearing a vulture crown or tiara – one of the animals with which she was related.

Khepri

Khepri, or Kheper, is one of the main Egyptian deities. Associated with the scarab beetle, which, by rolling balls of dung, is compared to the forces that move the Sun, Khepri gradually came to be considered as an incarnation of the Sun itself, assuming one of the aspects of this star. According to the myths, he was responsible for "rolling" the Sun – Ra's chariot – out of the Tuat at the end of the god's night journey, causing its daily rebirth. For this reason, Khepri was identified as a facet of Ra, his aspect as the Sun that breaks the dawn. Thus, Ra embodied the solar disk, Khepri the rising Sun and Atum the setting Sun.

Due to the characteristic of the scarab beetle of laying eggs in the dead bodies of animals, including other scarab beetles, the ancient Egyptians related Khepri to death and rebirth.

The scarab beetle god Khepri.

The god Khnum in the temple of Horus, Edfu, Egypt.

Khnum

Khnum, the god with the head of a ram, originally from southern Egypt and Nubia, dates back to pre-dynastic times. Khnum is a creator god who depicted the aspects that generated life and who contributed with other gods to regulate the floods of the Nile.

He was also connected to the creation of human beings, making his body and his Ka around himself with mud from the Nile. Khnum formed different Enneads in different cities. In Elephantine, Khnum formed a triad with the goddesses Satis and Anuket. In Esna, Ennead included, in addition to him, Satis and Neit.

An ancient legend, engraved on a stele from the Ptolemaic era, the "hunger stele", tells the origin of his cult. According to the account, in the reign of the pharaoh Djoser, Khnum stopped the waters of the Nile from flowing, causing a famine of seven years. Seeking to reverse the situation, Djoser made offerings to Khnum. Then, the deity appeared in a dream of the pharaoh and asked him to continue honoring him properly.

Khnum also depicted one of Ra's aspects, the sunset. According to this tradition, it was in this form that the Sun god started his journey through the Tuat.

Relief with the moon god Khonsu, his mother Hathor and his father Sobek, in the temple of Kom Ombo.

Khonsu

Khonsu was a god associated with the Moon. His name means "traveler", a reference to the moon's night trips across the sky. With Thoth, he embodied the passage of time. His sacred animal was the baboon, considered a lunar animal by the ancient Egyptians. Usually, he was depicted as a mummy with the symbol of childhood, a lock of hair. At times, he was depicted with a head of a falcon, like Horus, with whom Khonsu was associated as a protector and healer.

Maat

Maat, daughter (or, at times, mother or wife) of Ra and wife of Thoth, "the light that brings Ra to the world", was the ancient Egyptian goddess of truth, justice, righteousness and order. Maat was responsible for maintaining the cosmic and social order. The balance of the Universe, the relationship between its constituent parts, the cycle of the seasons, celes-

Maat, the goddess of cosmic order, in the temple of Osiris, in Abydos.

Isis and winged Maat, with Horus and queen Nefertari.

tial movements and religious observations, as well as fair dealings, honesty and trust in social interactions are aspects governed by this goddess. The principles of Maat were an integral part of Egyptian society and ensured public order. The fundamentals of maintaining order, followed by the Egyptians in obedience to Maat, became the basis of the law of ancient Egypt. If cosmic harmony was disturbed, this would reflect on the individual's life and, many times, on the destiny of the State. Because of this, a bad king could bring famine to the people. Thus, since the beginning of Egyptian civilization, the king was described as "Lord of Maat", who decreed, with his mouth, to Maat, who conceived in her heart the will of the pharaoh. It was up to the pharaoh to apply and enforce the law, to allow the maintenance of cosmic balance. Some pharaohs came to bear the title of Maat-Meri, or "beloved of Maat", emphasizing his role in the defense of the laws of universal harmony.

As Lady of Justice, it was Maat who validated the judgment of souls. Depicted as a young woman, she wore an ostrich feather (the feather of Maat) on her head, which she placed on the scale to weigh the heart of the dead in the judgment of Osiris.

As a civilizing god, and establisher of laws and knowledge, Thoth, patron of the scribes, is the husband of Maat. In an ancient text, Thoth is described as "the one who reveals Maat and recognizes Maat, who loves and gives Maat to the creator". Everyone should live according to Maat's precepts of truth and justice.

Maat was the sister of Isfet, the goddess of chaos, her opposite. Together, they balanced the positive and negative aspects of the Universe.

Negative Confessions to Maat

The Negative Confessions to Maat, found in the Papyrus of Ani, the best-known version of the Book of the Dead, were recited in religious meetings and written on sarcophagi and funerary monuments, and ended up constituting a kind of "commandments of righteousness", such as the decalogue is for Jews, Christians and Muslims.

I did not sin.

I did not steal with violence. I did not pilfer.

I did not murder man or woman. I did not steal grain.

I did not appropriate the offerings. I did not steal a god's property.

I did not utter lies.

I did not carry away food.

I did not utter obscene words.

I did not commit adultery; I did not sleep with men. I did not make anyone cry.

I did not feel useless remorse. I did not attack any man.

I am not a man of falsehoods.

I did not steal from cultivated land. I was not a snooper.

I did not slander.

I did not feel anger without just cause. I did not demoralize any man's wife.

I did not verbally demoralize any man's wife. I did not profane myself.

I did not master someone by terror. I did not break the law.

I was not angry.

I did not close my ears to true words. I did not blaspheme.

I am not a man of violence. I am not a conflict agitator.

> *I did not act or judge with undue haste. I did not press in debates.*
>
> *I did not multiply my words in speeches.*
>
> *I did not lead anyone astray. I did not do evil.*
>
> *I did not do sorcery or blaspheme against the king. I never stop the flow of water.*
>
> *I never raised my voice, spoke with arrogance or anger. I never cursed or blasphemed a god.*
>
> *I did not act out of evil anger.*
>
> *I did not steal bread from the gods.*
>
> *I did not divert the Khufu cakes from the spirits of the dead.*
>
> *I did not take bread from children or treat the god of my city with contempt.*
>
> *I did not kill the cattle belonging to a god.*

Mafdet

Like Maat, Mafdet was an ancient goddess associated with justice and royal power. In New Kingdom scenes she was seen as the executioner of evil creatures. Mafdet ripped out the hearts of evildoers, putting them at the pharaoh's feet, just as cats do when they leave at their owner's feet the rodents or birds they hunted. Thus, Mafdet is related to the punitive aspect of justice. However, in addition to this fierce side, Mafdet also had a protective side. She warded off venomous animals, seen as transgressors of the law of Maat. In this aspect, she was called the "Lady of the House of Life", in reference to the place where the sick were healed in ancient Egypt.

Mafdet was depicted as a feline, a woman with a head of a feline, or a feline with a head of a woman. In some images, she has her hair braided so that the tips end in scorpion tails.

Mafdet is depicted as a feline in the temple of Horus, in Edfu.

Later, her cult and attributes were incorporated by the goddesses Bastet and Sekhmet.

Mnevis

Like Apis, Mnevis was one of the sacred oxen of ancient Egypt, a black animal worshiped as a deity in the city of Heliopolis. Associated with the god Atum-Ra, his cult was instituted in the second dynasty, although he has probably been worshiped since pre-dynastic times. He was worshiped by all pharaohs, even by Akhenaten, who had forbidden the cult of any god, except Aten. As Aten manifested himself in Mnevis, the pharaoh allowed this god to continue to be worshiped.

Solar boat with serpent, symbol of the goddess Meretseger.

In the temples to Mnevis, its priests kept a sacred ox, whose movements were interpreted as an oracle. After its death, the bull was mummified, its organs placed in canopic jars and the sacred animal was buried in a necropolis destined for this purpose, near Heliopolis.

Meretseger was the serpent goddess. During the New Kingdom, this goddess became guardian of the tombs - it was believed that she attacked those who tried to pillage them. She lived on a pyramid-shaped mountain near the village where the royal tomb constructors lived during the New Kingdom. She attacked workers who committed crimes or lied, punishing them with blindness or poisonous stings, while healing those who felt regret. When the pharaohs stopped constructing their royal tombs in the Valley of the Kings in the 21st dynasty, her cult, which never surpassed the local scope, fell into decay.

Meskhenet

Meskhenet was the goddess of childbirth. Among her attributes, she shaped the Ka of all who would be born, ensured the birth and decided the fate of each being that was born. This goddess was also present at the judgment of souls, when the heart was weighed against the feather of Maat. If the soul was pure, Meskhenet assisted the person's entry into the afterlife. As the wife of Heryshaf, god of fertility, she also embodied the husband's attribute.

Montu

Montu is the god of war of the Egyptian pantheon, usually depicted as a man with a head of falcon, adorned with two feathers and a solar disk. In the early days of Egyptian civilization, he was depicted with the head of an ox. Montu was a solar god, associated with Ra (Montu-Ra), who represented the destructive aspect of the sun's heat. From the 11th dynasty, Montu assumed the attributes of god of war. Four pharaohs of this dynasty – established in Thebes, the greatest center of the cult of this god – were called Mentuhotep, that is, "Montu is satisfied", in honor to this deity. The Greeks, who dominated Egypt from the fourth century BC, associated Montu with Ares, their god of war.

Mut

Mut was the second wife of Amun and foster mother of Khonsu. In the 18th dynasty, when the cult of Amun became popular, Mut replaced the first woman of this deity, the goddess Amunet. She was depicted as a woman wearing a red or blue dress, wearing the serpent Uraeus and the double crown of Upper and Lower Egypt. At times, she was also depicted with the head of a lioness.

Nefertem

Nefertem, or Nefertum was a solar deity, god of the Sun and of perfumes, whose symbol was the lotus flower. With his parents, Ptah and Sekhmet, he forms an important triad. Over time, Nefertem was incorporated by Horus, forming a single entity. He was also seen as the manifestation of the god Atum as a child, who came out from the lotus flower that emerged from the primordial mound that emerged from the waters. He was sometimes depicted with the head of a lion or as a young man with a lotus-shaped crown, adorned with two feathers, sitting on a blossoming flower. Sometimes he appeared over a lion, carrying a saber.

Lioness goddesses in the Temple of Amun, in Karnak.

Nephthys embalming Tutankhamun's body.

Nephthys

Considered the lady of the shadows, she was the sister of Isis. Her Egyptian name, "Nebt-ha", means "Lady of the House", in reference to the house where the Sun returns at the end of the day, i.e., the night skies. In iconography, it is very hard to distinguish Nephthys from Isis, as both are depicted with the same characteristics, crowned with the head of a vulture, on which the solar disk also appears between the horns. For this reason, both are deities that distribute full life and happiness. Nephthys was the wife of Set, but had a son with Osiris – the god Anubis. However, there are different versions about the relationships between these gods. Nephthys is sometimes referred to as the wife of Osiris, while Isis is considered the wife of Set. Although she is Set's consort, she is not evil like her husband. Together with Isis, she mourned the murder of Osiris and cared for the body of the dead god. Because of this, she was seen as the guardian of the dead. She presides over the final moments of life, and to take the dead with kindness.

Nekhbet

Deity originally from the city of Nekheb, in Upper Egypt, today El-Kab – her name means precisely "That One of Nekheb" –, she protected births, especially those of kings. Some pharaohs wore her image on their crowns, as they believed that the amulet had the power to repel the sovereign's enemies. In iconography, she was depicted as a vulture, a woman with a head of a vulture, or a woman with the white crown of Upper Egypt (Hedjet).

The vulture goddess Nekhbet, protector of the pharaoh, in the temple of Medinet Habu.

Neith

Neith, or Nit, is the goddess of war and hunting, creator of gods and men, funerary deity and of inventions. Her cult already existed in the predynastic period, in which she was celebrated as a scarab beetle; later she was the goddess of war, hunting and the inventor goddess. Firmicus Maternus wrote in his book The Error of the Pagan Religions, that Plato stated that in the city of Sais, the Greek goddess Athena merged with Neith, due to the attributes of war and weaving, and they had the same symbolic animal: the owl. Neith was also a protector of the dead, as she was the one who invented the fabric, used both by the living and in the shroud of the dead.

Nut

Nut, the sky, was one of the most important Egyptian deities. Daughter of Shu, the dry air, and Tefnut, the moisture and

Priestess of the goddess Neith, goddess of war and hunting, in the temple of Dendera.

the clouds, she was the mother of Osiris, Set, Isis, and Nephthys, gave birth to them in a single birth. With her elongated body, covered by stars, she embraced Geb, the god of the Earth. In this way, she formed the arch of the celestial vault that extends over the Earth. In Egyptian iconography, she was often depicted as a cow, or as a woman with a sun disk over her head.

Osiris

Osiris, or Ausar in Egyptian, was one of the main deities of ancient Egypt. Son of Geb and Nut – earth and sky –, god of vegetation and life in the Beyond, the cult of Osiris dates back to the beginning of Egyptian civilization. Husband of Isis and father of Horus, he was the judge of souls, in the "Room of Two Truths", where the heart of the dead was weighed.

In early times, Osiris represented the forces of the earth and the plants. And like all vegetation gods, he was associated with death and rebirth. The first farmers created their myths from the observation of the cycle of the plants. Like the dead, the seed taken from the plant that was cut is buried to be born again. The idea of eternal life developed

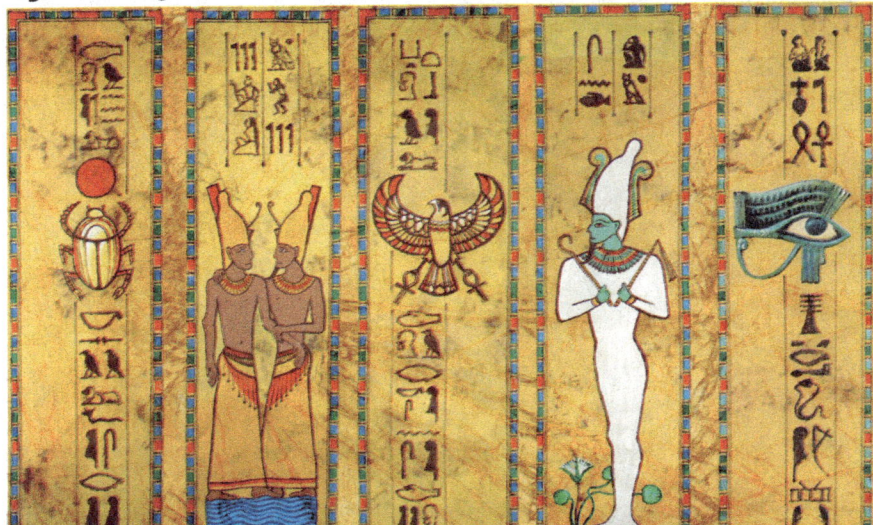

The god Osiris, with green skin, as the vegetation he governs, among Egyptian symbols.

from then on. Thus, Osiris was the deity that incarnated the Egyptian land and its vegetation, destroyed by the sun and drought, but always resurrected by the action of the waters of the Nile. He was a kind god who died a cruel death and who assured life and eternal happiness to all men and women. Osiris was also a civilizing deity, teaching human beings the knowledge necessary to the civilization, such as agriculture and the domestication of animals. Because of these characteristics, his cult spread throughout Egypt, and Osiris absorbed the attributes of the deities he incorporated, thus modifying himself through time.

Normally, he was depicted as a mummified man, wearing a white crown with two ostrich feathers and the false beard used by the pharaoh. His arms emerge from the mummy's bands and cross over his chest; in his hands, he bears the hekat staff and the nekhakha whip. In another common depiction, Osiris appeared as a lying mummy from whose body spikes emerged. The skin of the god was green or black, colors the Egyptians associated with fertility and rebirth. Rarely Osiris was depicted as an animal. When this happened, the god appeared as a black bull, a crocodile or a large fish.

The pharaoh Seti making an offering to Osiris, in the temple of this god, in Abydos.

The main cult centers of Osiris were Abydos and Busiris. In Abydos, every year, a procession was held in which the god's boat was carried by the faithful, in celebration of the god's victory over his enemies. As Osiris had been shredded by Set, the places where the cult of this deity was relevant, stated to have parts of the god's body. Osiris was also worshiped outside Egypt, in several Mediterranean cities, but never to the extent reached by the cult of his sister and wife, Isis.

During the Egyptian month of Khoaik (October-November), the "Mysteries of Osiris' ' were celebrated, when episodes of the myth were ritualized. For the Egyptians, it was in this month that Isis found the parts of Osiris' body.

Ptah

Ptah (probably pronounced "Pitaḥ") was the god of artisans and architects, equivalent to the Greek god Hephaestus. He was a member of the Memphis triad, with his wife Sekhmet and their son Nefertem. He was also considered the father of the vizier Imhotep, who designed the step pyramid of Saqqara. The constructor god Ptah was associated with stonework. Later he was combined with Seker and Osiris, creating the entity Ptah-Seker-Osiris. Husband of Sekhmet and, at times, Bastet, he was the father of Nefertem, Mihos, Imhotep and Maahes. In the arts, he was depicted as a mummified man with his hands holding a scepter adorned with symbols of life, strength and stability.

Ramesses II with the god Ptah, temple of Medinet Habu, near Luxor.

Statue of the sun god Ra.

Ra

Ra, or Re, the sun god, was another important deity of the ancient Egyptian religion. Identified with the midday sun, during the fifth dynasty, Ra became one of the most worshiped deities in Egypt. According to some traditions, all forms of life would have been created by Ra, who brought them to life by pronouncing their secret names. According to other versions, the human beings would have been created from Ra's tears and sweat.

In one of the stories about Ra, humanity schemes against the god. To punish the rebellious sons, Ra sent his eye, embodied in the goddess Sekhmet. But Sekhmet was too violent with her revenge and ended up becoming thirsty for human blood. Ra was only able to stop her by getting her drunk.

The main cult center of Ra was Heliopolis, as the Greeks called the Inun, or "Place of Pillars", of the Egyptians. Ra was associated with the sun god of that city, Atum, becoming Atum-Ra. Over time and in some places, Ra also merged with Horus, forming Re-Horakhty, or "Ra, who is Horus of the Two Horizons", sovereign entity of all parts of the created world – the sky, the earth and the underworld.

Like Horus, Ra was also associated with the falcon or the hawk and likewise, incarnated in the bull Mnevis. The cult of the sacred bull of Ra also had its center in Heliopolis.

Satet

Satet (or Satis) was the goddess of crops, and of the harmony that makes life possible in the environment. Thus, Satet represented the need for affinity with the environment for the realization of creation. Like other gods, she was also responsible for the floods of the Nile.

Sekhmet

Sekhmet, or Sakhet, "the mighty one", was the lioness goddess who brought revenge and disease, the punishment of Ra. She was the protector of Ra and the pharaoh. She was associated with the goddess Hathor, being, in fact, her vengeful aspect. According to this tradition, Hathor embraced Ra, absorbing his strength, and, in the form of a lioness, came down to earth to destroy humanity that schemed against the god. Paradoxically, she is also the patroness of doctors, as she brought the cure for the ills she herself spread.

Wife of Ptah and mother of Nefertem, the center of her cult was in the city of Memphis. She was depicted in iconography as a woman covered by a veil and with a head of a lion.

The mighty goddess of vengeance Sekhmet.

Serket

Serket, daughter of Ra, the scorpion goddess of Egyptian mythology, was the one who brought the cure for scorpion stings. Her most common depiction is that of a woman bringing on her head a scorpion with its tail raised, ready to sting. In some rarer depictions, Serket appears as a scorpion with a head of a woman, or as a serpent.

She was a goddess worshiped since the beginning of Egyptian civilization. It is believed that the Scorpion King would have worshiped this goddess. In the early days, she did not have the beneficial characteristics that she later acquired. She was the mother, or at times, wife of the serpent god Nehebkau, protector of royalty and who lived in the world of the dead. Because of this association, Serket was seen as the guardian of one of the four gates to the underworld, binding the dead with chains. When Nehebkau became a benevolent deity, Serket followed the same path.

Like Isis, Nephthys, and Neith, Serket kept the organs of the dead stored in canopic jars. Serket protected Qebehsenuef, one of the four

Gold statue of the protector goddess Serket, part of Tutankhamun's treasure.

Ruins of Agora and the temple of Serapis, in Ephesus, Turkey.

sons of Horus who were related to the intestines. In her aspect as a funereal goddess, she was the "Lady of the Beautiful Mansion", this mansion being the house where the mummification process took place.

Serapis

Serapis was a deity who arose from the syncretism between Egyptian and Hellenic gods. For this reason, her main temple was located in Alexandria, the city founded by Alexander the Great when he conquered Egypt. Under the Hellenic pharaoh Ptolemy Soter (366 - 283 BC), Alexander's general and founder of the Ptolemaic dynasty, several efforts were made to integrate the Egyptian religion with that of its Hellenic sovereigns. An anthropomorphic statue was created and officially proclaimed as equivalent to the extremely popular Egyptian god Apis. First called Aser-Hapi (i.e., Osiris-Apis), he became Serapis. Thus, on the Egyptian side, the god incorporated aspects of Osiris, and on the Greek side, he was related to Dionysus. Serapis is depicted as a man of mature age and serious face, wearing a beard and long hair. His attribute is the sacred basket, symbol of abundance, and the serpent of Asclepius, since he was also a god who brought healing.

Sechat

Seshat, or Seshet, was the goddess of science, patroness of writing, astronomy, architecture, mathematics and professionals in these areas. Her name means "the one who writes" and she was also called the "Lady of the Books" and the "Lady of the Constructors". She was present in the Egyptian pantheon since the Thinite time. Already in the second dynasty, she was celebrated in the ceremony of the foundation of temples and in the ritual of "stretching the rope", when the goddess, through a priest, presided over the necessary calculations for the construction of a new temple. As the goddess of writing and knowledge, she was associated with Thoth, appearing in some traditions as the wife of this god. While Thoth represented hidden, esoteric knowledge, Seshat represented esoteric, knowable knowledge. Her sister was Mafdet, goddess of justice.

Normally, Seshat was depicted as a woman dressed in leopard skin, used by priests in funeral rites, with her head adorned with a stylized papyrus plant or else, a star. In her hands she carried a style of reed and a palette, two instruments used by scribes in their work.

Set

Set was the spirit of evil, god of violence and disorder, betrayal, jealousy, envy, the desert, war, animals and serpents. Brother of Osiris and Isis, he was husband and brother of Nephthys. Set started caus-

Depiction of the god Set as a hippopotamus, one of the animals related to this god, on the outer wall of the temple of Horus, in Edfu.

ing evil at birth, when he ripped open his mother Nut's womb to get out. Originally, however, he helped Ra in his eternal fight against the serpent Apophis, incarnation of chaos. In that sense, Set was originally seen as a good god. However, with the development of the Empire and the fixation of historical facts in myths, Set started personifying the usurper, the one who did everything to get control of the gods and take the place of his brother Osiris. For this reason, he killed him and shredded his body. Then, he took the throne of Egypt. When Horus, son of Osiris, claimed the throne, Isis transformed herself into a beautiful young woman to seduce Set and thus achieve his confession before the Ennead (the family of gods) that her son Horus was, in fact, the heir by right, to the throne of Osiris. In the end, Horus ended up killing Set.

There are stories that record the betrayal of his wife Nephthys, who had a son with Osiris, the god Anubis.

Set was associated with several animals, such as the dog, crocodile, pig, donkey, scorpion and hippopotamus, a destructive and dangerous creature. As oxen were used to thresh cereal and knead grain, which, the Egyptians believed, contained the god Osiris, a recurring victim of Set, this animal was also associated with the god of chaos. A common depiction of Set was a part-ass, part-pig entity.

Shu
Shu, or Chu, is a primordial deity, god of dry air, male strength, heat, light and perfection. Together, Shu and his wife Tefnut, goddess of moisture and clouds, generated Geb and Nut – the earth and the sky. Shu is also the one who brought life with the light of day. He was also the creator of the stars, which human beings become after death. He was depicted as a man wearing a large ostrich feather on his head.

Sobek
Sobek, or Sebek, was the crocodile god of the ancient Egyptians, connected to the cult of the River Nile, the deification of water, its

The crocodile god Sobek.

powers of fertility and the protection during pregnancy. For hunting and consuming meat, he was also related to death. In his negative aspect, he was associated with Set. Sobek, in the form of a crocodile, was the one who devoured the heart of Osiris, connecting the reptile god to an idea of terror and annihilation. On the other hand, he also had a solar aspect. Like the sun, which every day rises in the sky bringing the day, so the crocodile comes out of the water. Thus, Sobek ended up being associated with the primordial god Ra (Sobek-Ra) and the resurrected Osiris.

He was depicted as a crocodile or, then, as a man with a head of a crocodile, sporting a crown adorned with two large feathers, the solar disk and one or more Uraeus – sacred serpents. His main cult centers were in Fayum and Kom Ombo, in a region where those reptiles were very abundant in the time of pharaonic Egypt. In the temples dedicated to Sobek there was often a tank with sacred crocodiles, which were mummified after death.

Sokar

Sokar, Seker or Sokaris, was a funerary god, depicted as a falcon or as a mummified man with the head of this bird sporting the white crown of Upper Egypt. From the fifth dynasty, he was identified with Ptah, main god of Memphis, originating a new entity, Ptah-Sokar. Due to his attribute of god of death, he was also associated with Osiris, becoming one of the aspects of this god. The "Texts of the Pyramids", the inscriptions made on the walls of the first pyramids, in Saqqara, report that Sokar was seen as Osiris, after he was murdered by his brother Set.

Because of his identification with Ptah, Sokar was a patron of the artisans. It was this god who produced the perfumes used in the ceremonies dedicated to the gods. However, Sokar also had a dark aspect. He was the guardian of the door of Tuat, the underworld, where he lived in a cave called Imhet, according to some traditions, feeding on the hearts of the dead.

An annual procession took place in Memphis on the 26th of Khoiak – the month corresponding to October/November. The god was carried on the shoulders of sixteen priests, in his sacred boat, Hennu. Sokar's consort was Sokaret, who had the same funerary attributes. At times, the goddess Sekhmet appears as Sokar's consort.

Sopdet

Sopdet was the personification of Sothis, probably the star Sirius. In fact, the name of this goddess refers to the brightness of Sirius – the brightest of the night. She is depicted in iconography as a woman with a five-pointed star over her head. As the flooding of the Nile occurred when Sirius appeared in the sky, in July, Sopdet was identified as a goddess of soil fertility. Sopdet is the consort of Sah, the constellation of Orion, and the planet Venus was, at times, considered her child. Over time, Orion started being identified as an aspect of Horus. For this reason – and because she was a fertility deity – she was also identified as a manifestation of Isis.

Tatenen

Tatenen was the god of the primordial mound that arose from the waters of chaos at the beginning of the created world. He was, therefore, a deity of creation. Tatenen represented the earth and was related to the mastabas and, later, the pyramids, since these funerary monuments were also seen as the primordial mound or a stairway that led to heaven – the kingdom of Horus. His father was the god Khnum, who created him on a potter's wheel with mud from the Nile. According to C. J. Bleeker, in his book Religions of the Past, he was seen as "the source of food, divine offerings and all good things". His kingdom was made up of the regions deep under the earth, "from where everything comes" – plants, waters and minerals. He was the personification of Egypt and, likewise, an aspect of the god of the earth, Geb. Like many Egyptian gods, Tatenen assisted the dead on their journey to the afterlife.

Originating from Memphis, where he was worshiped since archaic periods, he merged, in the Old Kingdom, with another god of this city, Ptah, forming the deity Ptah-Tatenen.

Taweret

Taweret, "The Great One", was the goddess of fertility and protector of boats and pregnant women. She was also a celestial goddess, the "Mysterious one of the Horizon". Taweret helped Horus in his fight against Set. She was the daughter of Ra and the right hand of Isis and Osiris. Due to her attribute of fertility, she was depicted in Egyptian art as a pregnant anthropo-zoomorphic figure, with black skin, hippopotamus head, with horns and solar disk, lion paws, crocodile tail and very large breasts. She also appeared in iconography as a pig.

Tefnut

Tefnut, or Tefnet, is a creation goddess related to Egyptian cosmogony. Daughter of Ra, sister and wife of Shu, mother of Geb and Nut, and grandmother of Osiris, Isis, Set and Nephthys. She personified moisture and clouds and her attributes are generosity as well as

The lioness goddess Tefnut in relief in the temple of Horus, in Edfu.

gifts. As her brother Shu wards off hunger from the dead, she wards off thirst. In iconography, she is depicted as a woman, at times with the head of a lioness, crowned with the sun disk and the serpent Uraeus.

Thot

Thoth, a god with the head of an ibis, had as attributes the esoteric knowledge and magic. His cult center was Hermopolis. The Hellenic invaders related Thoth to their god Hermes and, from this syncretism, a civilizing entity was born, Hermes Trimegistus, the "Thrice Great". Considered in his time "the messenger of the gods", Hermes would have given the Egyptian people the precepts of civilization, with its sciences and its culture. It would also have been Hermes who implanted the occult sacred tradition, its rituals and the very Mysteries of Isis and Osiris. The Greeks claim that Hermes bequeathed 42 sacred books, including the Ancient Egyptian Book of the Dead. He also founded schools of wisdom attached to major sanctuaries, where priests taught medicine, astronomy, astrology, botany, agriculture, geology, natural sciences, mathe-

Thoth, the god of esoteric knowledge and writing, in a relief in the temple of Ramesses II, in Abydos.

matics, music, architecture, sculpture, painting, and political science. Thus, Hermes would have been a true civilizer.

Wadjet

Wadjet was the goddess of vegetation, patroness of Lower Egypt – the Nile Delta region. Her name means "The Green One", in an allusion to the plant of the papyrus, created by this goddess and given as a gift to humanity. Wadjet played a relevant role in the Egyptian mythological cycle as the wet nurse of Horus, when Isis entrusted her son to her, hiding him in the swamps of the Delta to escape the murderous usurper Set.

She was depicted as a woman with a head of a serpent, sporting a red crown, a symbol of Lower Egypt. When the artist alluded to her aspect as a defender of royalty, Wadjet was portrayed as a woman with a head of lioness. She was also symbolized by a winged serpent, or a snake coiled in a papyrus basket.

Wepwawet

Wepwawet, or Upuaut, was a late god, a war deity, whose cult was centered in Assiut, in Upper Egypt. Wepwawet was the scout, the one who goes ahead of the Army, opening and clearing the way. For this very reason, he appears in iconography as a wolf on the prow of a solar boat. He became a symbol of the pharaoh, being seen as the king's protector. In this aspect, one of his attributes was to accompany the sovereign on hunts.

As a scout, an entity of war, Wepwawet also had a funeral function, guiding the souls of the dead through the Tuat, the world of the afterlife. He also assisted in the ritual of opening the mouth, when the priest released, in this ritual act, the soul of the dead. Due to his resemblance to the jackal and his aspect as a deity of death, he was associated with Anubis and, in some places of the cult, he was considered the son of this god. In others, he was the son of Set.

In iconography, he was depicted as a wolf – at times, a jackal – with white or gray fur, or he was portrayed as a man with the head of these animals, dressed and equipped as a soldier, armed with a mace and a bow.

Wepwawet, the scout of the gods, protector of the pharaoh.

Main Egyptian Gods

Egyptian Name	Greek Name	Greek Deity	Symbol	Attributes
Amen	Amun	Zeus	Ram	Creator god
Kratos	Inpu	Hermes	Dog	God of war
Amunet		Athena	Frog	Goddess of the occult, and the power that is not extinguished
Ankt			Bee, beetle	Goddess of war
Anit			Woman's body	Goddess of war
Anuket	Anukis		Gazelle	Goddess of the Nile and water
Hep	*Apis*		Ox	God of fertility
Aten	Aton		Sun	Creator solar god
Temu	Atum		Phoenix or ram	Creator solar god

The Big Book of Egyptian Mythology

Egyptian Name	Greek Name	Greek Deity	Symbol	Attributes
Bastet	Bast	*Artemis*	Cat	Lunar goddess protector of the house
Keb	Geb	Cronus	Earth	Creator god
Hep	Hapi		Nile River	God of floods
Hut-Hor	Hathor	Aphrodite	Cow	Goddess of love and happiness
Hor	Horus	Ares	Falcon	God of war
Imhotep	Imouthes	Asclepius	Wisdom	God of medicine and scribes
Ast	*Isis*	Demeter	*Tree*	Goddess of magic
Khepri			Scarab beetle	Self-created solar god
Khnum	Chnoubis		Ram	God of Creation
Khonsu			Falcon	Lunar god, protector of the sick
Maat			Cosmic harmony	Truth, justice and harmony
Meskhenet			Woman or cow	Goddess protector of motherhood and childhood
Menu	Min	Pan	White bull or lion	Lunar god of fertility and vegetation
Montu	Monthu		Falcon	Solar god. Also god of war
Mut		Hera	Vulture, cow or lioness	Mother goddess, origin of the creator
Nebet-Het	Nephthys		Buzzard	Goddess of rivers
Nekhbet		Eileithyia	Vulture	Protective goddess of births and wars
Net	Neith	Athena	Owl, bee, beetle, etc.	Goddess of war and hunting
Nut	Nut	Rhea	The celestial vault	Sky goddess, creator of the universe
Asar	Osiris		The Great Judge	God of resurrection
Ptah		Hephaestus		Creator god. Also god of the artisans
Ra		Zeus	Falcon	Solar god, demiurge
Satet	Satis	Hera	Antelope	Goddess protector of the pharaoh
Sekhmet	Sacmis		Lioness	Goddess of war
Serket Heru	Selkis		Scorpion	Goddess protector of magic
User-Hep	Serapis	Zeus	Bull	Official god of Egypt and Greece
Seshat				Goddess of writing and the calendar
Suty	Seth	Typhon	The desert	God protector/destroyer of evil
Shu		Agathodaemon	The atmosphere. Lion	God of air and light
Sobek	Suchos	Helios	Crocodile	God of the Nile
Sokar	Sokaris		Falcon	God of darkness and Tuat

The Egyptian Gods

Egyptian Name	Greek Name	Greek Deity	Symbol	Attributes
Sopdet	Sotis		The star Sirius. Dog or buzzard	Mother and sister of the pharaoh
Tatenen			The primordial mound. Ram or serpent	God creator and of what is born under the earth
Taweret	Taouris		Hippopotamus	Goddess of fertility and protector of women
Tefnut	Tefnet		Lioness	Warrior goddess and humility
Djehuty	Thoth	Hermes	*Ibis or mandrill*	God of wisdom and writing
Wadjet	Uto	Leto	The burning heat of the Sun. Snake or lioness	Goddess protector of the pharaoh
Wepwawet	Ophois	Ares	Black dog or jackal	God of war and Tuat

Bibliography

E-REFERENCES

BUDGE, E. A. Wallis. *Legends of the Gods: The Egyptian Texts, Edited with Translations.* Available in: http://www.gutenberg.org/cache/epub/9411/pg9411-images.html. Acessado em 09.03.2016.

HERÓDOTO. *An Account of Egypt. Translation of G.C. Macauley.* Available in: https://www.gutenberg.org/files/2131/2131-h/ 2131-h.htm. Acessado em 13.02.2015.

BIBLIOGRAPHIC REFERENCES

BLAINEY, Geoffrey. *Uma Breve História do Mundo.* Curitiba: Fundamento, 2009.

BLEEKER, C.J. *Religions of the Past vol. I.* Boston: E.J. Brill, 1969.

CAMPBELL, Joseph. *O Herói de Mil Faces*. Translation of Adail Ubirajara Sobral. São Paulo: Cultrix/Pensamento, 1995.

DURANT, Will. *Heróis da História – Uma Breve História da Civilização da Antiguidade ao Alvorecer da Era Moderna*. Translation of Laura Alves and Aurélio Barroso Rebello. Rio de Janeiro: Ediouro, 2002.

ELIADE, Mircea. *O Conhecimento Sagrado de Todas as Eras*. Translation of Luiz L. Gomes. São Paulo: Mercuryo, 1995.

FAURE, Élie. *History of Art: Ancient Art*. Nova York: Garden City, 1921.

HUXLEY, Aldous. *A Filosofia Perene*. Translation of Octavio Mendes Cajado. São Paulo: Cultrix, 2006.

JAGUARIBE, Helio. *Um Estudo Crítico da História*. Translation of Sérgio Bath. São Paulo: Paz e Terra, 2001.

PLATÃO. *Diálogos (O Banquete – Fédon – Sofista – Político)*. Translation of José Cavalcante de Souza, Jorge Paleikat e João Cruz Costa. São Paulo: Abril Cultural, 1972.

ROBERTS, J.M. *A Short History of the World*. Oxford: Oxford University Press, 1997.

SMITH, Huston. *As Religiões do Mundo*. Translation of Merle Scoss. São Paulo: Cultrix, 2002.

**CHECK OUT OUR
RELEASES HERE!**

Camelot
EDITORA

Made in the USA
Columbia, SC
14 April 2025